Advance Praise for *Twilight's Last Gleaming*

"Todd Starnes is a fierce defender of freedom and a great patriot. He has seen, and understands, what is happening to our country like few others—his book is absolutely terrific, a must read!"

—President Trump

"Todd Starnes articulates Joe Biden's radical attempt to destroy American society both politically and culturally like no one else can. America is at a crossroads, and this book provides a beacon of hope and aspiration to embrace our nation's core values and reclaim our founding principles. A must read for anyone who values freedom, liberty, and the future of America."

—Marsha Blackburn, US Senator

"Todd Starnes has been sounding the alarm that America is under attack from within. For more than two decades, he has been the trusted voice on the frontlines of the battle to save this country. *Twilight's Last Gleaming* is a roadmap for patriots who want to save America."

—Congressman Jim Jordan

"Todd Starnes is one of the most eloquent and courageous voices in the country today declaring a way forward to restore America to moral and spiritual greatness. Once again, Todd delivers a compelling roadmap for conservatives to reclaim our nation's future as we approach the most consequential election in history. I highly recommend this book."

—Ralph Reed, Founder and Chairman, Faith & Freedom Coalition

"*Twilight's Last Gleaming* is a wake-up call to the church. Todd Starnes lays out the case for Christians to engage the culture. Even though the nation is in the throes of moral chaos, Todd shows us the path forward—if we are willing to take it."

—**Pastor Jack Hibbs,** Calvary Chapel Chino Hills, California

"With the Radical Left seeking to dismantle the foundation of America stone by stone, Todd Starnes' *Twilight's Last Gleaming* is a rallying cry to defend our conservative values and a must-read for anyone who believes America is worth fighting for."

—**Timothy Head,** Executive Director, Faith & Freedom Coalition

"I have long appreciated Todd's reporting on stories that bring to light the current infringements on religious liberty, systemic attacks on the traditional family, and growing trends of anti-patriotism here in the United States. And *Twilight's Last Gleaming* does not disappoint. In his signature wit and with down-home humor sprinkled in, Todd delivers another excellent book calling conservative Americans to take a courageous stand for the historic values of our nation."

—**Dr. Paul Chappell,** Pastor of Lancaster Baptist Church and President of West Coast Baptist College

"Todd Starnes is one of the top conservative voices in the country. He knows well how imperative it is we have strong fighters defending our Constitution and the American way of life. Todd is a true patriot."

—**Congressman David Kustoff**

"*Twilight's Last Gleaming* is a sobering look at where the policies of the Left have taken our nation. Todd's book shines a bright light on the darkness and illustrates how to truly make America great again."

—Dr. Robert Jeffress, First Baptist Church Dallas, Texas

"Todd Starnes serves as a once-in-a-generation voice for the American conservative movement. In *Twilight's Last Gleaming,* Todd fearlessly tackles the critical issues that will define the future of our country and confronts the truth behind the Radical Left's extremist agenda that threatens our freedom. This is a must-read book for any patriot who holds our conservative values dear, and is dedicated to preserving the cherished principles that define our great nation."

—Congresswoman Diana Harshbarger

ALSO BY TODD STARNES

Culture Jihad: How to Stop the Left from Killing a Nation
Our Daily Biscuit: Devotions with a Drawl

TWILIGHT'S LAST GLEAMING

CAN AMERICA BE SAVED?

TODD STARNES

A POST HILL PRESS BOOK
ISBN: 978-1-63758-478-1
ISBN (eBook): 978-1-63758-479-8

Twilight's Last Gleaming:
Can America Be Saved?

Cover design by Joseph Huntley

Post Hill Press
New York • Nashville
posthillpress.com

Published in the United States of America
2 3 4 5 6 7 8 9 10

TWILIGHT'S LAST GLEAMING

CAN AMERICA BE SAVED?

TODD STARNES

A POST HILL PRESS BOOK
ISBN: 978-1-63758-478-1
ISBN (eBook): 978-1-63758-479-8

Twilight's Last Gleaming:
Can America Be Saved?

Cover design by Joseph Huntley

Post Hill Press
New York • Nashville
posthillpress.com

Published in the United States of America
2 3 4 5 6 7 8 9 10

To my family, the staff at Starnes Media Group, and the bold ambassadors for Lady Liberty who listen to my radio show every day at noon from border to border and coast to coast across the fruited plain.

TABLE OF CONTENTS

1

DARTH BRANDON AND THE TEMPLE OF DOOM

"It is impossible to rightly govern a nation without God and the Bible."

—Origin Unknown

JUST AFTER THE disastrous midterm elections in 2022, a listener called into my national radio show with an interesting question.

"When did the United States cross the Rubicon?" Bill from Tulsa, Oklahoma, asked. In other words, when did we pass the point of no return?

I think it happened sometime between the Federal Bureau of Investigation raiding Mar-a-Lago and Cracker Barrel putting plant-based sausage on its menu.

Since President Biden placed his hand on what we thought was a Holy Bible and took the oath of office, our nation has jettisoned down a path that is leading to socialism.

He promised to protect our nation from all enemies, foreign and domestic. But we had no idea that he would consider all of us gun-toting, Bible-clinging, flag-waving constitutionalists as the enemy.

Since Inauguration Day, the president has waged a relentless war on Christians, Jews, America First conservatives, and pro-lifers.

The FBI was weaponized to target Biden's political enemies. And there is considerable evidence that agents were involved in the planning and execution of the January 6, 2021, attack on the US Capitol. They infiltrated Catholic churches and labeled evangelical Christian organizations as domestic hate groups.

A militant band of transgender terrorists has waged war on churches and Christian schools, vowing to destroy the traditional family. Pronoun-confused radicals have turned public school classrooms into grooming gulags where children are filled with LGBTQIA propaganda.

Biden shut down our churches but let the liquor stores and whorehouses remain open. He ordered small business owners to close their doors while letting big box retailers sell their goods.

Democrats across the fruited plain have been systematically curtailing our civil liberties. And I have been documenting this unconstitutional crackdown daily on my radio program.

Governors and mayors tried to shut down gun sales in the Commonwealth of Virginia and in Los Angeles. They declared war on churches in Louisiana, Mississippi, Michigan, Kentucky, and Illinois.

Worshipers were slapped with $500 fines in Greenville, Mississippi, and a New Jersey police chief threatened to arrest anyone who showed up at a prayer vigil in a hospital parking lot.

Kentucky's governor ordered state police to gather license plate information from Easter Sunday worshipers and ordered all Christians who attended to quarantine for fourteen days.

But perhaps the most egregious crackdown happened in Michigan where Governor Gretchen Whitmer ruled during the China Virus pandemic with an iron fist.

"If you're not buying food or medicine or other essential items, you should not be going to the store," the governor told ABC 13 News.[1]

"Farmers markets may also be barred from selling seedlings for fruits and vegetables," the Michigan NPR affiliate reported.

"Currently there is a ban on all plant sales at the market. So, that is a big portion of our May market and so we might have to limit particular vendors at that time," Fulton Street Market executive director Rori Jean Trench told the radio station.[2]

"The petty tyrant Michigan leader Governor Whitmer mandates that citizens may not travel to their own second residences, may not buy garden seeds or a can of paint. Such govt overreach represents an affront against common sense and our principles of liberty," political pundit Steve Cortes said.[3]

The Michigan Farm Bureau told radio station WSJM that the governor should reconsider her decision and reopen nurseries.[4]

"If they lose this opportunity to sell their products, it is the entire year's worth of income that is lost for this industry," spokesperson Audrey Sebolt told the radio station.

---

1 13 On Your Side Staff, "New Stay at Home Order Closes Garden Centers, Other Parts of Grocery Stores," 13 On Your Side, April 10, 2020, https://www.wzzm13.com/article/news/health/coronavirus/stay-at-home-order-closes-garden-centers-other-parts-of-grocery-stores/69-f9f79a8f-3ae3-4057-afc0-13ab14b8ab52.

2 Lester Graham, "Garden Centers at Large Stores Must Close under Governor's Order," Michigan Radio, April 10, 2020, https://www.michiganradio.org/health/2020-04-10/garden-centers-at-large-stores-must-close-under-governors-order.

3 Steve Cortes (@CortesSteve), "The petty tyrant Michigan leader @GovWhitmer mandates that citizens..." Tweet, April 11, 2020, https://twitter.com/cortessteve/status/1248984069045714946.

4 "Michigan Farm Bureau to Governor Whitmer: Reclassify Greenhouses, Garden Centers as Essential," News/Talk/Sports 94.9 WSJM, April 10, 2020, https://www.wsjm.com/2020/04/10/michigan-farm-bureau-to-governor-whitmer-reclassify-greenhouses-garden-centers-as-essential/.

In a statement, the Farm Bureau wrote, "It's disappointing to hear that the governor's new EO [executive order] does not allow the sale of flower and vegetable plants in a safe manner. It will be a total loss for this industry if they are not allowed to sell their plants over the next eight weeks."[5]

In Washington, DC, Mayor Muriel Bowser—also a Democrat—declared that fish markets and farmers markets were no longer essential businesses. Anyone who wanted to operate a market during the pandemic had to obtain a mandatory government-issued waiver.

So, let's review: the Democrats wanted to take away our guns, our freedom to assemble, and our religious liberty. And they wanted to take away our ability to grow our own food?

Remember what former secretary of state Henry Kissinger once said: "Whoever controls the food supply controls the people."

New York City Mayor Bill de Blasio used the pandemic as cover to declare war on churches and synagogues, announcing an immediate ban on corporate worship.

"Everyone has been instructed, if they see worship services going on, they will go to the officials of that congregation, inform them they need to stop the services and disperse," the mayor said during a press briefing.

"If that does not happen, they will take additional action up to the point of fines and potentially closing the building permanently," he stated.[6]

---

5 Genevieve Grippo, "Greenhouses Unable to Sell in Michigan under Extended Order, Banking on May Business," News Channel 3, April 11, 2020, https://wwmt.com/news/local/greenhouses-unable-to-sell-in-michigan-under-extended-order-banking-on-may-business.

6 Shane Vander Hart, "De Blasio's Blatantly Unconstitutional Threat," Caffeinated Thoughts, March 31, 2020, https://caffeinatedthoughts.com/2020/03/de-blasios-blatantly-unconstitutional-threat/.

He actually ordered police to forcefully shut down peaceful churches.

This is not America—this is a police state.

Dr. Robert Jeffress, the pastor of First Baptist Church, Dallas, Texas, predicted the Biden administration would be hostile to people of faith.

Pastor Jeffress delivered a bombshell news report on my radio show. It turned out the Internal Revenue Service was about to start targeting Christians—and he had the evidence.

He said pastors who preach about marriage and biblical sexuality will face the possibility that their tax-exempt status could be revoked.

Most recently, a ministry called Christians Engaged was flagged by the IRS, their tax-exempt status denied because they followed—and I quote—"Bible teachings affiliated with the Republican Party."

"They're going to say, 'When you preach certain things or allow certain things to be said from your pulpit that is politics and therefore disqualifies you from tax-exempt status,'" said Jeffress. "That is being tested right now by the IRS. I have absolute impeccable inside sources that there is some test cases going on right now."[7]

It's strange to imagine such a thing—but the Democrats have an ugly history of using the IRS as their attack dog. During the Obama administration, they actually audited Billy Graham—America's preacher.

If Billy Graham was fair game—the rest of us are doomed.

---

7 Todd Starnes, "STARNES: Jeffress Says He Has Evidence IRS Will Target Churches," Todd Starnes, March 14, 2022, https://www.toddstarnes.com/opinion/starnes-jeffress-says-he-has-evidence-irs-will-target-churches/.

And that brings me to a speech Biden delivered that has become known as the "Darth Brandon Address from the Temple of Doom."

Fuhrer Biden announced to the world that the greatest threat to the United States is not Russia or China or Iran. He said the greatest threat to our nation is conservatives.

"Donald Trump and the MAGA Republicans represent an extremism that threatens the very foundations of our republic," the Fuhrer declared with fists clenched and squinty eyes.

Independence Hall was bathed in blood-red lights in a scene that seemed more appropriate for Nazi Germany or *Star Wars*.

The president's message was clear: anyone who opposes his agenda should be labeled an extremist. It's only a matter of time before conservatives are targeted for violence in the streets.

"There is no question that the Republican Party today is dominated, driven, and intimidated by Donald Trump and the MAGA Republicans, and that is a threat to this country," Biden said.

"MAGA Republicans do not respect the Constitution. They do not believe in the rule of law. They do not recognize the will of the people.

"They refuse to accept the results of a free election. And they're working right now, as I speak, in state after state to give power to decide elections in America to partisans and cronies, empowering election deniers to undermine democracy itself.

"MAGA forces are determined to take this country backwards—backwards to an America where there is no right to choose, no right to privacy, no right to contraception, no right to marry who you love.

"They promote authoritarian leaders, and they fan the flames of political violence that are a threat to our personal rights, to the pursuit of justice, to the rule of law, to the very soul of this country.

"They look at the mob that stormed the United States Capitol on January 6th—brutally attacking law enforcement—not as insurrectionists who placed a dagger to the throat of our democracy, but they look at them as patriots.

"And they see their MAGA failure to stop a peaceful transfer of power after the 2020 election as preparation for the 2022 and 2024 elections.

"They tried everything last time to nullify the votes of 81 million people. This time, they're determined to succeed in thwarting the will of the people.

"That's why respected conservatives, like Federal Circuit Court Judge Michael Luttig, has called Trump and the extreme MAGA Republicans, quote, a 'clear and present danger' to our democracy."

Conservatives condemned the president's violent remarks.

"Is Joe about to announce the roundup of all the Trump voters?" former Arkansas governor Mike Huckabee wrote on Twitter. "Pure hate speech if there ever was one."[8]

Sen. Ted Cruz (R-TX) accused Biden of tearing the country apart.

"Tonight, Joe Biden vilified millions of Americans in a divisive & angry speech that was detached from the reality of his political failures. He isn't actually interested in restoring the soul

---

8 Gov. Mike Huckabee (@GovMikeHuckabee), "Is Joe about to announce the round up of all the Trump voters?" Tweet, September 1, 2022, https://twitter.com/GovMikeHuckabee/status/1565494783442915330?lang=en.

of the nation, he's only interested in pitting his fellow Americans against one another," Cruz said.[9]

Biden accused conservatives of being fascists when in fact his own administration has behaved like the fascists. It was Democrats who shut down our businesses, our schools, and our church houses. It was Democrats who told Jews they could not bury their dead. It was Democrats who punished Christians for singing hymns.

And it was a Democrat who styled himself as a modern-day Hitler in front of the birthplace of our great nation.

A full transcript of Fuhrer Biden's remarks can be found on the White House website.[10]

Franklin Graham, the great American evangelist, unloaded on President Biden's "Darth Brandon" address to the nation.

"The White House is trying to defend President Biden offending over half the American people. The President campaigned on uniting the country, not dividing it," Graham wrote.[11]

"Senator Tim Scott said it well: 'In his soul-crushing "soul of the nation" speech, the president threw half the country back into Hillary Clinton's basket of deplorables. Anyone who refuses to go along with his radical agenda that's bankrupting the country is a threat. Anyone who stands up for religious liberty is an

---

9 Ted Cruz (@tedcruz), "Tonight, Joe Biden vilified millions of Americans in a divisive & angry speech that was detached from the reality of his political failures," Tweet, September 1, 2022, https://twitter.com/tedcruz/status/1565529714940313600?lang=en.

10 Joseph R Biden, "Remarks by President Biden on the Continued Battle for the Soul of the Nation," The White House, September 1, 2022, https://www.whitehouse.gov/briefing-room/speeches-remarks/2022/09/01/remarks-by-president-bidenon-the-continued-battle-for-the-soul-of-the-nation/.

11 Franklin Graham (@Franklin_Graham), "The White House is trying to defend President Biden offending over half the American people," Tweet, September 2, 2022, https://twitter.com/Franklin_Graham/status/1565877159381590017.

extremist. Anyone who is a voice for voiceless and vulnerable unborn babies is a danger to democracy. That's the picture Biden painted of America. But his illustration of our country and her people couldn't be more disconnected from reality.'"[12]

Franklin Graham, the president of the Billy Graham Evangelistic Association and Samaritan's Purse, conveyed the feelings of most Americans who were appalled by Biden's dark and ominous speech delivered amid the blood-red backdrop of lights with US Marines nearby.

> President Biden said that MAGA threatens the very foundation of our republic. Really? I want to see America great again. I want to see America as a leader, as a place for people who desire liberty and justice for all. I don't want to see this country turned into a socialist country. I don't want to see it fail. Does believing in freedom, justice, opportunity, less taxes, and smaller government make me an extremist? Absolutely not. The ones who are extremists are the ones who want to take that away from us! Ronald Reagan campaigned to Make America Great Again. Does that make him an extremist? President Biden is trying to vilify and demean conservative, freedom-loving Americans who do not support the failing and economically unsound policies of his administration. This is just further dividing our nation.

12 Sen. Tim Scott, "Biden Just Painted a Soul-Crushing Vision of America That Does Not Reflect The Country I Know and Love," Fox News, September 2, 2022, https://www.foxnews.com/opinion/biden-painted-soul-crushing-vision-america-reflect-country-know-love.

> Ultimately, America can only have true greatness through God. The blessings of this nation have come from the hand of God. We need to turn to Him. We need His help, His direction, and His healing.[13]

My suspicions are that Barack Obama and Susan Rice had a role in orchestrating President Biden's "Darth Brandon" speech. This is simply a continuation of the Democrat Party's attempt to dehumanize conservatives. They have called us bitter, irredeemable, deplorables, dregs of society, and fascists.

Even CNN pundits have admitted that Biden's vilification of conservatives was over the top and unpresidential.

I predict the abusive language is only going to become more vile and detestable as we head into the 2024 presidential election. It's as if they want to instigate some sort of altercation or confrontation. But conservatives must not take the bait. We can punch back at the ballot box. And we must punch back hard.

I was half-expecting to be dragged out of bed by government agents the morning after the address. That's one of the reasons why I always wear pajamas—and MyPillow slippers.

And if you don't believe the foundations of our nation are under assault, consider this:

For quite some time I've been documenting the radicalization of American public school classrooms. Our public schools have been overrun by radical academics who are driving the mas-

---

13 Franklin Graham, "Tonight President Biden said that MAGA threatens the very foundation of our republic," Facebook, September 1, 2022, https://www.facebook.com/FranklinGraham/posts/621915662637365/?paipv=0&eav=Afar2JMFeHVaeLRyD8eAoMo-FuKf7MOrBl_3hmxR-E4G-wsy3F0ECS0dPzMMeHGeUhg&_rdr.

sive social and cultural change that's occurring in our society. Educators, inspired by former president Barack Obama, have been fundamentally transforming our nation from the comfort of their classrooms.

The latest evidence came courtesy of Project Veritas, a nonprofit journalism organization that exposes corruption and dishonesty in public and private institutions.

Project Veritas captured Advanced Placement government teacher Gabriel Gipe on an undercover video boasting about his intention to turn your kids into Communist revolutionaries.

"I have 180 days to turn them [students] into revolutionaries…Scare the f*ck out of them," said Gipe, a teacher at Inderkum High School in Sacramento, California.

And so far, Mr. Gipe's nefarious plan is working. His classroom is a museum for radicals—from the rainbow flag and a portrait of Chairman Mao to a giant Antifa flag.

"I have an Antifa flag on my [classroom] wall and a student complained about that—he said it made him feel uncomfortable. Well, this [Antifa flag] is meant to make fascists feel uncomfortable, so if you feel uncomfortable, I don't really know what to tell you. Maybe you shouldn't be aligning with the values that this [Antifa flag] is antithetical to," he told Project Veritas.

The teacher also keeps tabs on the political leanings of his students. Over the years his students have gone even further to the left.

His goal is not to teach Advanced Placement government. His goal is to replace our government and fundamentally transform America.

"What can we do now to root out this culture that keeps perpetuating hyper-individualism, hyper-competitiveness, capitalist exploitation and consolidation of wealth...I do think that it's important to understand that as an extension of an economic revolution, [the Chinese Communist Party] were changing the base, and then they went to change the superstructure. You cannot change one without the other. You can't have cultural shifts without the economic shift, and vice versa," he said.

And he's not the only teacher at Inderkum High School who has turned his classroom into a Communist training camp.

"There are three other teachers in my department that I did my credential program with—and they're rad. They're great people. They're definitely on the same page," he said.

Folks, I've been warning about this for years—unless we root out the anti-American, anti-Christian radicals inside our classrooms, we will not have meaningful change in America.

One more note: when Project Veritas confronted Sacramento school officials, they were the ones thrown out of the building.[14]

And if you need further proof, consider how Democrats dealt with a Baptist church in California that refused to comply with the China Virus shutdown.

A message was posted on the front door of the North Valley Baptist Church in Santa Clara:

"Cease and Desist."

The Santa Clara County Counsel officially ordered the megachurch to shut its doors because it was in violation of the law.

The congregation had been accused of holding indoor services, failing to ensure that speakers wore face masks, and singing.

14 "Project Veritas Just Dropped This Video about Antifa Teachers," Public School Exit, September 1, 2021, https://www.publicschoolexit.com/news/project-veritas-just-dropped-this-video-about-antifa-teachers.

Yes, good readers, the church stands accused of singing hymns and spiritual songs.

"North Valley Baptist is failing to prevent those attending, performing and speaking at North Valley Baptist's services from singing," read the letter. "This activity is unlawful."[15]

Let that sink in for just a moment, folks. Congregational worship is against the law in California.

"The county understands that singing is an intimate and meaningful component of religious worship," the letter read. "However, public health experts have also determined that singing together in close proximity and without face coverings transmits virus particles further in the air than breathing or speaking quietly."

Santa Clara County acknowledged in its cease and desist order that they had been sending agents into the church to spy on the congregation during worship services.

"The county demands that North Valley Baptist immediately cease the activities listed above and fully comply with the Risk Reduction Order, the Gatherings Directive, the State July 13 Order and the State guidance," the letter threatened. "Failure to do so will result in enforcement action by the county."

Now, it's important to remember that North Valley Baptist Church is in the United States of America, not the Soviet Union.

The idea that government agents could infiltrate the congregation and post a cease and desist order on the front door of the church house is unthinkable. And the mere suggestion that

15 Andrea Morris, "'We Answer to a Higher Power': 2 More CA Churches Fined for Gathering, Ordered to Stop Singing," Christian Broadcasting Network, August 25, 2020, https://www2.cbn.com/news/us/we-answer-higher-power-2-more-ca-churches-fined-gathering-ordered-stop-singing.

pastors of the church could face some sort of legal penalty is outrageous.

Fortunately, Pastor Jack Trieber and the congregation of North Valley Baptist Church did what any red-blooded, Bible-believing, American patriot would do—they held church on Sunday.

"You can't have any law against assembling in God's house," the pastor told the church on Sunday. "None."

"I know we have a Constitutional right to worship, but we have a Higher Power that we answer to," he said. "I have a biblical mandate."

Pastor Trieber said the church has done its best to follow the mandates of local and state leaders. And he pointed out that they have implemented social distancing policies within the building.

"We have obeyed authority in this church. We've always obeyed authority. But when local authority begins to disregard [God's] authority, we go with this book right here," he said pointing at the Bible.

Pastor Trieber said he bears no ill will towards Santa Clara leaders or Governor Gavin Newsom. And he is well aware that there is a remote possibility that he could suffer severe consequences for his decision to preach from the pulpit.

"If they close us down in the middle of the service, I'm just going to go over to the park," he said.

But Pastor Trieber also offered a warning to state and local lawmakers.

"Politicians, do not move against the church," he said.

It's not the first time in world history that authors and artists and pastors and political pundits have been silenced. Look no further than 1930s Germany to see what happens when your ideology clashes with the ruling class.

A great darkness swept across the world, and I fear we may be in for some very difficult days.

On January 7, 2021, the political director of ABC News literally called for the cleansing of Trump supporters—a tweet he later deleted.

But still, he said it.

Biden told us darkness was coming to America. And he delivered on that promise.

As we near the end of his term in office, our nation is less free. Christians and conservatives have been the targets of brutal attacks by the government and the alphabet activists.

They have already announced their intentions to declare an all-out war on the traditional American family. The Democrats will seek to shut down our businesses and our church houses.

If you are a follower of Almighty God, you need to be prepared for these days of persecution. But as Christians, we must be courageous, knowing that Light dispels the darkness. And one day, morning will return to America.

In the following pages, I'm going to provide you with the evidence that our schools, our families, and our churches are under attack. Our way of life, our very existence as a sovereign nation is under assault.

Some of the chapters will make you laugh, and some will make you cry. Other chapters will curdle your Froot Loops, and a few might make you cuss like a deacon at a Wednesday night church business meeting.

And that's okay—except for the cussing part.

I know that many of you want a quick fix, but that's just not how it's going to work. It's going to take some time. Hemorrhoids don't just go away overnight. And unfortunately, our nation is suffering from a raging case of the 'roids.

So, pour yourself a Baptist Martini or a glass of the House Wine of the South and settle in for an eye-popping glance at what the Left has done to America.

And for you Methodists out there, a Baptist Martini is a Diet Coke with a wedge of lemon. And for you Greek Orthodox folks, the House Wine of the South is a frosty glass of Luzianne Iced Tea.

And based on what you're about to read, I'd make it a double.

2

DID BIDEN'S HATRED OF REPUBLICANS GO TOO FAR?

NOT TOO LONG after President Biden delivered his infamous "Darth Brandon" address in the dark of night in Philadelphia, a young man was killed in North Dakota. Many on the right believed eighteen-year-old Cayler Ellingson was killed because he happened to be a conservative. And many believe Biden's rhetoric led to the young man's murder.

President Trump suggested as much during an appearance on my radio show.

"They say he [the North Dakota killer] got a lot of language, a lot of his hatred from maybe that speech," Trump said, referring to Biden's "Darth Brandon" address in front of Independence Hall in Philadelphia.

Since 2016, the Democrats and mainstream media have waged an ugly smear campaign against Republicans.

They've used their platforms to accuse conservatives of being deplorable and bitter, white supremacists, dregs of society, Christian nationalists—and most recently, the president of the United States called Trump supporters fascists and extremists.

Here are some thoughts I shared during an opening monologue not long after Ellingson was murdered:

> I want to address a story that really should be discussed across the nation right now. And it's an issue that should be the top story in the news cycle right now, but it is not. And if it had been anyone other than a Republican teenager, this would be a national news story.
>
> Of course, we're talking about this horrible story out of North Dakota where a grown man used his vehicle to mow down an eighteen-year-old boy because this boy happened to be a Republican. And we now know because the man confessed to the crime, this man who was set free on $50,000 bail—I guess they have a George Soros district attorney in North Dakota.
>
> But the man who committed the crime said he did so because he believed that Cayler Ellingson was a religious or was rather a Republican extremist. Well, now the North Dakota Highway Patrol is coming out. And by the way, the guy said that Ellingson was getting his friends together and they were going to chase after the guy. And the highway patrol says, no, there's no evidence of that at all. There's no evidence that this young man, an eighteen-year-old boy, was an extremist.
>
> But it's interesting, because the guy who committed this atrocity, this heinous crime, snuffed

out the life of an eighteen-year-old Republican child. The man who did that used the exact same language that President Biden has been using and, quite frankly, used last night again when Biden called out every MAGA Republican.

Now, you might remember a few weeks ago, he said he had to come back after the infamous Darth Brandon speech in front of the blood-red Independence Hall. And his staff had to walk all of that back. And even Biden himself had to come out and say that he wasn't talking about all MAGA Republicans.

But last night, in front of this crowd of Democrats, he said he was talking about MAGA Republicans, all of them. So, he said he's not just talking about Trump. He's talking about all MAGA Republicans. And we know for a fact that the killer was using the language that was spewing out of Joe Biden's decrepit mouth. We know that for a fact.

We know that over really the past seven years now, the Democrats and the media have been smearing and slandering conservatives and Trump supporters. They have called us every name out of the book, and this really goes all the way back to 2007, when Barack Hussein Obama, at a gathering in San Francisco, talked about all you people who live in the Rust Belt, Ohio and Pennsylvania, West Virginia. He said, you people, you clung to your guns, and you clung to your religion.

Hillary Clinton picked up the attacks, calling us irredeemable deplorables. Nowadays, you've got Joe Biden out there and the Democrats calling us white supremacists and literally the dregs of society. By the way, that's what Joe Biden called all of you Christians who believe that marriage is between one man and one woman: dregs of society. That's what Joe Biden called you.

And now you have the woke evangelicals out there smearing people, accusing Christians of being evil because they love their country. And in recent days, you've had the president of the United States out there calling Trump supporters fascist and extremist. And that was the word, the verbiage used by this killer of this eighteen-year-old boy in North Dakota.

May I just point something out here for just a moment? There has been no media coverage of this outside of this radio program and Fox News. Where has the media been? Can you imagine? And I just and I don't even want you to imagine this, but for the sake of our conversation today, because we don't wish ill on anybody, we want everybody to be able to live their lives and claim their American dream, whether they're a

Democrat or a Republican or a Libertarian. We don't wish ill, we don't wish harm on anyone. But these Democrats and the language coming out of this White House, there is no doubt in my mind that they want to see dead Republicans in the streets.

We're living in a very dangerous time in American history. And this sort of violent political rhetoric that's coming from the White House and coming from the mainstream media, it endangers all of us. There's a great big target on anybody who happens to be a conservative these days. But imagine for just a moment, for the sake of the argument here, that this had been a Trump supporter who took his car and intentionally mowed down Democrat supporters of Joe Biden. And just imagine the media coverage of that for a moment. Every single news agency in the world would be parked and camped out in North Dakota, every single one of them, and rightfully so. It's a huge story. If someone is killed because of some sort of a political motive, then yeah, that's going to be a big national story, no doubt about it.

But not this time. Not this time. Not for Cayler Ellingson. It's almost as if this crime never happened. I mean, we all know that the mainstream media is biased. We get that. We know that the fix is in. But this should alarm all of you. Because this story should be used as an opportunity to tone it down, to take it down a few notches. But that's not what Biden has done. Two times, two times since this kid was killed, Biden has been out there ratcheting up the rhetoric. And that's why I do believe that they are hoping that their followers take the bait and target again.

Joe Biden, actually, yesterday at this speech, Joe Biden said that the Republicans were going to be guilty for blood in the streets. What have we been talking about for ages on this radio program, that when the Democrats do that, when they make a charge about Republicans, typically they are projecting, and they are the ones guilty of whatever they're accusing the other side of doing. The only people that are being left bloodied and beaten in the streets, ladies and gentlemen, happen to be conservatives, happen to be Trump supporters. But they don't want to have that conversation.

The mainstream media is not honest enough to actually call out the Democrats for any of this stuff. Not a single national news reporter had the courage, had the moral fortitude to actually ask the Biden administration to ask them whether or not they regret the language they're using or if they wanted to retract the language they're using, if they wanted to walk back the language they're using, nobody did that. Nobody did that. Because you see, in Biden's America, all lives do not matter. When it comes to the Democrats, our lives don't matter.

If you disagree with the Biden administration, it's not just that you're a fellow American who has a difference of opinion. No, you become the enemy. That is a very dangerous thing.

3

BUTTER MY BUTT AND CALL ME A BISCUIT

I RECEIVED AN urgent call around 2 a.m. in my New York City apartment. On the line was Uncle Jerry back home in the Mid-South. It was during the early days of the China Virus pandemic. His voice sounded somewhat panicked.

"You have to get back to Memphis lickety-split," he said. "We've got big problems down here. It's a state of emergency."

I wasn't all that convinced, seeing how Memphis is controlled by a raging mob of progressive Democrats who think criminals are victims and white bread is racist. They *always* have problems.

One of my favorite stories in this book is how city leaders appeased a mob of race grifters by renaming Confederate Park and replacing a statue of Jefferson Davis with a giant afro-pick and black power fist. Yessir, Memphis is all about racial reconciliation.

But then Uncle Jerry dropped the bombshell.

"Todd, the barbecue joint is serving tofu," he shouted into the phone. "THEY'RE BARBECUING TOFU."

Well, butter my butt and call me a biscuit.

What in the name of Sweet Baby Ray's had those godforsaken, heathen Democrats done to my beloved city?

I told Uncle Jerry I'd be in the Bluff City by sundown.

I called the Delta Diamond Medallion desk and explained my predicament, and they, too, sounded just as horrified. I believe the agent's exact words were, "They're barbecuing what? Sweet Jesus."

I quickly packed my bags, hopped into the elevator, and rushed out onto Flatbush Avenue in downtown Brooklyn. My driver flung my bags into the trunk, and we scurried off to LaGuardia Airport. And by scurry, it took about ninety minutes to travel the ten miles to the airport. Rush hour traffic.

When I arrived back home, I rushed over to the barbecue restaurant and discovered that Uncle Jerry had been correct—barbecue tofu was on the menu. And somebody had taken the sugar out of the sweet tea.

I can't bring myself to share the name of the establishment, but they actually boasted that they were known for their "world famous barbecue tofu."

Now, I'm not so sure I'd be proud of highlighting something like that below the Mason-Dixon Line. Most bona fide meat-and-three's down in Dixie would never have tofu on the menu. And on the off chance the chef was a Democrat, they'd at least have the decency to make folks eat it out back—away from the meat-eating customers.

I researched the joint online and discovered they also offered something called a "southern fried tofu sandwich." "Pickle-brined tofu battered and fried to perfection, served on a brioche bun," the restaurant proudly declared.

Even if I wanted to explore the vegan culinary scene, I'm not too sure the tofu would make it past my tonsils. There's nothing "southern" about tofu—no matter how you fry it.

As I scrolled through the menu, I noticed they had an "animal-friendly" menu—which is code for "we cater to the soy boy, man bun crowd."

This particular restaurant was owned and operated by a disciple of Fuhrer Fauci who demanded that all diners had to show their vaccination papers. Staffers, too, had to be vaccinated.

"There are plenty of restaurants hiring, so no one has to go without a job," the owner told the *Daily Memphian* newspaper. "But we're going to have full compliance here."[1]

In other words, no clot shot, no job.

My philosophy during the pandemic was to double down on my civil liberties. I never ordered my staff to wear a mask. Nor did I force them to get a vaccine. My advice was and remains to seek the counsel of Almighty God and your personal physician.

And I was more than disappointed to see that so many back home in Memphis had surrendered their civil liberties based on "feeling" safe.

But the situation in Memphis was even more grim than I could have imagined.

I decided to collect my thoughts by taking a stroll through Shelby Farms, one of the nation's largest urban parks and home to an impressive herd of bison.

I had wanted to sit in one of the swinging chairs on the waterfront of Hyde Lake, but staffers had roped off the area with yellow crime scene tape.

---

1 Jennifer Biggs, "Three Local Bars, Restaurants to Require Proof of Vaccination," Daily Memphian, August 7, 2021, https://dailymemphian.com/section/metro/article/23381/local-bars-restaurants-vaccination-proof-covid.

It turns out that Fuhrer Fauci had ruled that fresh air and brisk walks were a leading cause of spreading the China Virus. And butt sweat might lead to an outbreak—hence the ban on swinging chairs.

So, I wandered around the nearly vacant parkland until a worker approached me and ordered me to mask up.

"But there's nobody around," I protested to no avail. No mask, no exercise.

I reckoned they were afraid I might infect the bison. So, I went back downtown.

I had taken up residence in the beloved Peabody Hotel, the South's Grand Hotel. It was all but empty because of the pandemic. Just me and the ducks paddling away in the marble fountain.

The following morning, I woke up early to take in the sunrise on the rooftop and then proceeded to the restaurant for a sausage biscuit.

"No biscuits," the waitress said.

"You've sold out? But I'm the only person in the hotel."

"No, sir. We stopped serving biscuits before the pandemic. Would you like a bagel?"

Lord, Jesus. The South got invaded—again. And they took away our biscuits. Oh, the scourge of the China Virus pandemic.

But things were getting just as bad back in Brooklyn. I received word that the city had run out of cream cheese. New Yorkers had nothing to schmear on their bagels.

"Without cream cheese, there is little reason to eat a bagel," a Grub Street writer mourned in a story titled, "Life Without Cream Cheese."[2]

---

2 Alan Sytsma, "Life without Cream Cheese," Grub Street, December 6, 2021, https://www.grubstreet.com/2021/12/there-is-no-substitute-for-cream-cheese.html.

"Sure, there is butter. And tofu cream cheese. And plenty of acceptable bagel sandwiches require no cream cheese at all. But for the people who *want* cream cheese—most people, of course—this is an accept-no-substitutions-type situation," the writer wrote.

The *New York Times* reports that the shortages are being blamed on supply chain issues.[3] In other words, it's President Biden's fault that many Upper West Siders will have to eat dry bagels at Zabar's.

"I've never been out of cream cheese for 30 years," Joseph Yemma, the owner of F&H Dairies told the *Times*. "There's no end in sight."

"It's been very weird things, and always the same story," said Christopher Pugliese, the owner of Tompkins Square Bagels in the East Village. "All of us behind the scenes, when you go into the shops, we're all struggling to patch things together."

Pugliese told the *Times* he had gotten a call from his dairy supplier telling him that the eight hundred-pound order he was expecting on Friday would not be arriving.[4]

"I was like, 'What am I going to do this weekend?'" Mr. Pugliese said. "Four people just told me they can't get me cream cheese."

To help put this in perspective for our Southern readers—imagine being told there was no butter for your biscuits.

I thought about driving down to Oxford, home of Ole Miss and Square Books. I figured if anybody might have a biscuit, it

3 Ashley Wong, "How a Cream Cheese Shortage Is Affecting N.Y.C. Bagel Shops," *New York Times*, December 4, 2021, https://www.nytimes.com/2021/12/04/nyregion/cream-cheese-shortage-nyc-bagels.html.

4 Ibid.

would be in Mississippi. But it turns out much of the Magnolia State was also under the control of Fuhrer Fauci.

Meet John Currence, the owner of City Grocery Restaurant Group in Oxford and a raging liberal who once called President Trump a moron.

"Just put on your freaking mask and shut the hell up," he wrote on Instagram. "Stop playing like this is about freedom. You can't smoke in our restaurants, you have to wear shirts, kids can't drink, you can't man-handle my staff, you can't carry a gun, so why is a MASK an 'infringement' on your freedom?"

For the record, yours truly is not responsible for giving the James Beard Award-winning chef a bad case of indigestion.

"We need to be perfectly clear about this. This is not about individual freedom. This is about the social contract," he said. "This is about each one of us doing the best we can to take care of one another—to take care of our communities—to take care of our country and our world."

Currence told television station WREG that his Instagram rant was meant to be an "inspirational message."[5]

"Let's be very clear, this virus is still out there. It is still a very significant threat to everyone's health," he said in the video. "There is no cure for this virus that is out there. This virus is still imminent. This virus is still a threat."

If he's that worried about a virus without a known cure, why reopen his restaurants at all? Why expose his staff and diners to unnecessary risks if he truly believes the virus is still a threat?

---

5 Stacy Jacobson, "Mississippi Restauranteur John Currence on Refusals to Wear Face Masks: 'This Is Not about You,'" WREG Memphis, May 28, 2020, https://wreg.com/news/mississippi-restauranteur-john-currence-on-refusals-to-wear-face-masks-this-is-not-about-you/.

"For those of you who feel inconvenienced or embarrassed by wearing masks, get over yourselves," he said. "This is not about you. This is not about freedom."

Now that sounds like something the Iranian ayatollahs would tell ladies who want to venture outside without wearing a head covering.

Chef Currence describes himself as an "opinionated husband," and his Twitter page is filled with opinions—several rather critical of President Trump and his handling of the China Virus.

Even though the chef is a face diaper Nazi, I heard he made great fried chicken and biscuits. So, I figured I'd mask up. But there was one significant problem. For the life of me, I couldn't figure out how to eat sweet tea-brined fried chicken without removing my face diaper.

He's also not a fan of Mississippi's Republican US senators.

"It is not your place to question decisions that individual businesses make about what they expect in the way of behavior of people to protect the greatest number of folks they can," Chef Currence declared on Instagram.

Now, that's a fair point.

Chef Currence absolutely has a God-given, constitutionally-protected right to run his business as he sees fit.

And likewise, Mississippians have a God-given and constitutionally-protected right to butter their biscuits someplace else.

So, I returned to the Peabody and settled into a seat in the lobby near the ducks to contemplate the great injustices inflicted on us not so much by the China Virus but by Fuhrer Fauci.

The Bible says we should count our blessings and consider it all joy—even when there are no biscuits on the supper table. I reckon I'll be joyful, but I'm still not eating barbecue tofu.

4

JACK AND JILL RAN UP THE HILL AND CAME DOWN GENDER NEUTRAL

"Boys are boys from the beginning. Girls are girls right from the start."

—Mister Rogers

ERIN HEALY IS a Democrat state representative from South Dakota. She believes that children are safer with the government than with their parents.

"Extremist group Family Heritage Alliance said this morning that the safest place for kids are in families that have a married mom and dad. What a dangerous and un-American belief," she wrote on Twitter.[1]

I wish I could tell you that Representative Healy's statement was an outlier within the world of politics, but it is not.

Washington State lawmakers have passed legislation that would allow the state to legally hide runaway children from

1 Admin, "According to Rep. Healy, Family Heritage Alliance Is an 'Extremist Group,'" Family Heritage Alliance, February 21, 2023, https://www.familyheritagealliance.org/according-to-rep-healy-family-heritage-alliance-is-an-extremist-group/.

their parents if the parents don't consent to their child's "gender transition" or abortion. No allegation of abuse in the household is required.

"This bill also applies to children from other states who may travel thousands of miles for such procedures not available to them at home, cementing Washington as a 'sanctuary state'[2] for runaway teens. And if that wasn't enough, the bill allocates up to $7.5 million of Washington taxpayers' money to the Office of Homeless Youth Prevention and Protection to provide grants to organizations to pay for gender transition and abortion procedures," Sarah Parshall Perry wrote in an essay published by The Heritage Foundation.[3]

"The horrifying reality is that Washington's bill is not the first of its kind, nor is it likely to be the last. Within a few months of Washington's introduction of the bill, California—already a 'sanctuary state' for minors seeking so-called gender transition—fell in line and introduced a similarly devastating bill.[4] The California proposal[5] would allow a minor to obtain 'gender-affirming' mental health interventions without parental knowledge or consent," she added, calling it the "stuff of parents' nightmares."

---

2 Ari Hoffman, "Washington Moves to Become Latest Sanctuary State for Child Sex Changes," The Post Millennial, March 2, 2023, https://thepostmillennial.com/washington-moves-to-become-latest-sanctuary-state-for-child-sex-changes.

3 Sarah Parshall Perry, "Stuff of Parents' Nightmares: Washington State Bill Hides Runaway Kids from Transgender-'Unsupportive' Parents," The Heritage Foundation, April 18, 2023, https://www.heritage.org/gender/commentary/stuff-parents-nightmares-washington-state-bill-hides-runaway-kids-transgender.

4 Assembly Bill 665, California Legislative Information § (2023), https://leginfo.legislature.ca.gov/faces/billTextClient.xhtml?bill_id=202320240AB665.

5 Wesley J. Smith, "California Bill to Exclude Parents from Children's Mental-Health Care," National Review, April 14, 2023, https://www.nationalreview.com/corner/california-bill-to-exclude-parents-from-childrens-mental-health-care/.

Fortunately, parents are fighting back thanks to activist groups on social media. Libs of Tik Tok has done a tremendous job exposing the radicalization that's been happening in public school classrooms.

The number of teachers who think they know better than parents is staggering. The Libs of Tik Tok page found one video of an unhinged educator who says she will never stop shoving propaganda down the orifices of her students.

"If you want to stop me you're gonna have to f***ing kill me," the teacher wrote as she parodied a scene from the popular Netflix show, *Ozark*.

"I will say gay and I will protect trans kids," the unnamed teacher said.

Perhaps the teacher would be much more effective if she taught the kids how to read and write instead of teaching them to be confused about their pronouns.

Children at a Texas grade school were forced to participate in a gay pride celebration. It happened at Doss Elementary School in Austin, preschool through fifth grade.

The kids staged a gay pride parade—waving rainbow-colored posters and chanting about pride, according to video obtained by Libs of Tik Tok.

But it's what happened inside the classrooms that alarmed parents.

Preschoolers were put into circles to discuss issues like families and respecting differences.

Teachers told the children not to tell their parents what they learned during Pride Week.

"What we say in this classroom stays in this classroom." That's what the teachers told the four- and five-year-olds.

Older students were also warned to keep their classroom discussions confidential.

"I want to thank everyone for participating in the Circle and for sharing your thoughts and listening to each other with respect," read a document for third through fifth graders. "Please remember that we agreed to keep what happened in this Circle confidential."

Now why in the world would public school teachers issue such an order?

I can't imagine any reason for parents to be kept in the dark about what their kids learn inside a taxpayer-funded classroom—or any other classroom for that matter.

And that should especially hold true when teachers are spewing LGBT propaganda into the minds of a bunch of four-year-olds behind closed doors.

Even though Hollywood and the world of academia have embraced the alphabet activists, most Americans have not.

The American people overwhelmingly reject transgenderism: the notion that men can become women and vice versa.

A new Rasmussen Report shows that 75 percent of American adults believe there are only two genders: male and female.[6]

Among black Americans the numbers are even higher—nine out of ten—82 percent say God created male and female.[7]

Even a majority of Democrats reject transgenderism.

---

6 "Most Americans Side with J.K. Rowling: Only Two Genders," Rasmussen Reports, December 27, 2021, https://www.rasmussenreports.com/public_content/lifestyle/public_surveys/most_americans_side_with_j_k_rowling_only_two_genders.

7 Neil Munro, "Poll Shows Black Americans Reject Transgender Claim by 10 to One." Breitbart, December 28, 2021, https://www.breitbart.com/health/2021/12/28/poll-shows-black-americans-reject-transgender-claim-by-10-to-1/.

The outrage is greatest among feminists and conservatives—making strange bedfellows in a fight for women's rights.

But the alphabet activists don't care. They are focused on grooming children inside our taxpayer-funded classrooms. And so far, they have been very successful.

"I've been wanting to do this for the past two years. Sorry, I'm like, so emotional and I just haven't had the courage to do it out of fear of just judgment, mostly from their parents, but I had these kids in fourth grade and now I have them in sixth and I'm sending them to middle school. And I love these kids so much and I trust them and they make me feel safe and I know they love me and it just felt right. And I did it and it was so beautiful. They had so many questions, which I loved. They wanted to learn and they wanted to learn about me, and they were so eager and a few of them clapped, which was so precious," one teacher said on Tik Tok.

My friend, Congressman Matt Rosendale of Montana, called the teacher's comments strange and disturbing.

"For the teacher to be looking for affirmation and support from the fourth and fifth and sixth graders and having those discussions—this is not about education," he said on my national radio program. "That's what I call pedophilia."

The congressman believes, as I do, that there is a war on the traditional family in America.

"I'm really just a firm believer that the hard, hard left is trying to destroy our families. They're trying to keep us from practicing our faith, and they're trying to brainwash our children. And everyone needs to stand up and say, we're not going to tolerate it. The emperor is not wearing clothes. And you can say what you want about me, but the truth is the truth, and we're just not going to put up with that anymore," he said.

GAY MEN'S CHORUS SAYS THEY'RE COMING FOR YOUR CHILDREN

The San Francisco Gay Men's Chorus is facing a firestorm of controversy over a sickening music video that featured choir members saying they were coming after the children of presumably heterosexual Americans.

NotTheBee.com first reported this disturbing nonsense.[8]

Soloists sang gleefully about converting straight children.

The video has since been removed—but it's as creepy and predatory as you might imagine.

Now far be it for me to tell you how to respond to this Broadway-style show tune, but it might be a very good idea to take them at their word.

May God protect the children, especially the children of San Francisco.

LAWMAKER WANTS TO ARREST ANTI-GAY PARENTS

A Virginia lawmaker floated a trial balloon the other day that stunned parents.

Delegate Elizabeth Guzman wanted to reintroduce legislation that would charge parents with a felony or misdemeanor if they did not affirm their child's sexual orientation and gender identity.

Guzman is a social worker in real life.

---

8 Doc Holliday, "San Fran Gay Choir Literally Sings 'We're Coming for Your Children' in New Music Video," Not the Bee, July 7, 2021, https://notthebee.com/article/the-san-fran-gay-choir-says-its-coming-to-convert-our-kids?fbclid=IwAR1QW37FB2bwrnBrPXksXQ7Q-YksI-bOMLoWMvlikFrtLc-KmBjGTjROQ3U.

"As a social worker & mom of 4, I will always fight to protect LGBTQ children from abuse," Guzman tweeted.[9]

She said her legislation is more about educating parents and telling them that you can't abuse your kids because they are gay.

"Using Child Protective Services to intimidate and threaten parents is abhorrent," said Hung Cao, a 2024 Republican congressional candidate in Loudoun County. "Elizabeth Guzman has overstepped her responsibility as a Virginia delegate by proposing a law that, to its core, seeks to separate children from parents."[10]

Governor Glenn Youngkin said children belong to their parents, not the Commonwealth of Virginia.

"What we saw is a clear statement of what the progressive liberals believe. They believe if parents try to be parents they should be investigated," Youngkin told television station WJLA. "We saw Attorney General Garland out of the US government investigating parents for standing up at board meetings. We saw my opponent last year stand up and say parents don't have the right to see what's being taught in classrooms."[11]

Taken to the extreme, a parent could actually be arrested and thrown in jail for refusing to acknowledge that their child is a dinosaur or a Shetland pony.

---

9 Elizabeth Guzman (@guzman4virginia), "As a social worker & mom of 4, I will always fight to protect LGBTQ children from abuse," Tweet, October 14, 2022, https://twitter.com/guzman4virginia/status/1580973478542704641.

10 Michael Martz, "Scott Rejects Guzman's 'Abuse' Proposal for Retaliation Against Transgender Kids," *Richmond Times-Dispatch*, October 14, 2022, https://richmond.com/news/state-and-regional/govt-and-politics/scott-rejects-guzmans-abuse-proposal-for-retaliation-against-transgender-kids/article_2fc6a016-b306-546a-9bd3-6acb99bf6f0e.html.

11 Nick Minock, "Gov. Youngkin Slams Guzman's Bill That Would Make It Illegal to Not Affirm LGBTQ Children," WJLA/ABC 7 News, October 18, 2022, https://wjla.com/news/crisis-in-the-classrooms/glenn-youngkin-responds-blasts-elizabeth-guzman-bill-affirming-gender-identity-lgbtqia-child-student-governor-parents-charges-education-protective-services-politics-abigail-spanberger-yesli-vega-virginia-election.

TRANSGENDER CITIZENS TO GET TAXPAYER CASH

Transgender citizens of San Francisco are now eligible for $1,200 a month in taxpayer-funded cash.

This is all part of a program that will give fifty-five transgender residents a monthly stipend for up to eighteen months. The only qualification is that you are confused about your preferred pronouns.

Mayor London Breed says the program will provide economically marginalized transgender people with a guaranteed income.

If you are a straight person who is down on his luck and in need of cash—tough cookies. You are not eligible.

"Our Guaranteed Income Programs allow us to help our residents when they need it most as part of our City's economic recovery and our commitment to creating a more just city for all," Breed said in a statement.[12] "We know that our trans communities experience much higher rates of poverty and discrimination, so this program will target support to lift individuals in this community up. We will keep building on programs like this to provide those in the greatest need with the financial resources and services to help them thrive."

Back when I was a kid, there were just two genders. God made little girls and little boys.

What I found to be extremely interesting is that San Francisco has now identified ninety-seven new gender options.

Among the new genders are xenogender, tomboy, polygender, and graygender—I guess that's what they're calling the senior citizens nowadays?

---

12 Madison Hirneisen, "San Francisco Launches Guaranteed Income Program for Transgender Community," The Center Square, November 16, 2022, https://www.thecentersquare.com/california/san-francisco-launches-guaranteed-income-program-for-transgender-community/article_d60e007a-6600-11ed-9d23-57f2b376ccc9.html.

Butch, brotherboy, demi-boy, and stud are also listed as new genders. No muffin, just stud.

I was surprised to learn that snowflake and pajama boy did not make the list.[13]

San Francisco's latest initiative is even more perverse than the behavior of Sodom and Gomorrah. And we all know how that story turned out.

COUNSELOR PUNISHED FOR OPPOSING SEX-CHANGE SURGERIES

Marissa Darlingh is a grade school counselor in Milwaukee.

She spoke at a public rally against sex-change surgeries and transgenderism.

She said that she would never allow students to be exposed to gender identity ideology. And she used profanity to make her point.

Instead of saluting Ms. Darlingh, the Wisconsin Department of Public Instruction launched an investigation.

She's been accused of immoral conduct by publicly voicing her opposition to the transgender movement.

And if she's found guilty, the state could revoke her license as an educator.

"According to a report and video submitted by a community member, you participated in an event in Madison on April 23, 2022, in which you identify yourself as an elementary school counselor," read a letter to the counselor obtained by Daily

---

13 "Guaranteed Income for Trans People (GIFT) Program Application," Lyon Martin Community Health and the Transgender District, accessed September 23, 2023, https://www.giftincome.org/_files/ugd/40a234_fa065a88cf9b481bbae6e47c5598270c.pdf.

Wire.[14] "You are on video saying 'f*** transgenderism.' You state you do not believe children should have access to hormones or surgery."

The Wisconsin Institute for Law and Liberty (WILL) says they will sue the state if she is suspended or her license is revoked.

"The state is, quite simply, trying to punish a public-school counselor for her views on gender ideology," WILL's Luke Berg told Daily Wire. "This is a classic, clear-cut, violation of the First Amendment and the state can expect a federal lawsuit if it proceeds."

They say Ms. Darlingh has a constitutional right to say whatever she wants in a public gathering—regardless of her status as a teacher.

DISNEY BOSS WANTS FIVE-YEAR-OLDS TO LEARN GAY SEX

The former head of the Walt Disney Company said he supports teaching kindergarten students about transgenderism and gay sex.

Bob Chapek announced his opposition to Florida's falsely named "Don't Say Gay" bill. In reality, the legislation would ban schools from teaching sexuality to children in kindergarten through third grade.

Mr. Chapek also pledged to donate $5 million to radical LGBT organizations.

In response, Florida Governor Ron DeSantis threw down the hammer, blasting what he called "woke corporations" like Walt Disney.[15]

14 Greg Wilson, "'F*** Transgenderism': Elementary School Counselor Probed for 'Immoral' Opposition to Kids' Sex Changes: Report," The Daily Wire, May 26, 2022, https://www.dailywire.com/news/f-transgenderism-elementary-school-counselor-probed-for-immoral-opposition-to-kids-sex-changes-report.

15 Solange Reyner, "DeSantis Blasts 'Woke' Disney CEO over Parental Rights Bill Criticism," Todd Starnes, March 11, 2022, https://www.toddstarnes.com/politics/desantis-blasts-woke-disney-ceo-over-parental-rights-bill-criticism/.

"In Florida, our policies got to be based on the best interest of Florida citizens, not on the musing of woke corporations," DeSantis told Fox News.

"If that's the hill they're going to die on, then how do they possibly explain lining their pockets with their relationship from the Communist Party of China? Because that's what they do, and they make a fortune, and they don't say a word about the really brutal practices that you see over there at the hands of the CCP," DeSantis added.

The governor says Walt Disney made a fortune off being family-friendly and catering to families and young kids.

But Disney is not family friendly—and they haven't been for a very long time. They have long carried water for radical LGBT activists. They have bullied and intimidated government leaders for decades—but not Ron DeSantis. The Florida governor actually stood up to the bullies wearing mouse ears. The question is whether moms and dads will do the same.

Walt Disney must be rolling over in his grave.

His beloved company has been overrun by a bunch of perverted sex and gender revolutionaries who are hell-bent on indoctrinating your child.

In the latest episode of Disney Junior's *Muppet Babies*, the beloved Gonzo appears in a dress and announces that he has a new name: "Gonzo-rella," Out.com reports.[16]

The pro-gay website saluted the "Cinderella" twist for its "powerful message of love and acceptance to gender-variant kids everywhere!"

---

16 Mey Rude, "'Muppet Babies' Just Celebrated Gender-Variant Kids in the Best Way," *Out*, July 26, 2021, https://www.out.com/television/2021/7/26/muppet-babies-just-celebrated-gender-variant-kids-best-way.

I previously mentioned the San Francisco Gay Men's Chorus.[17] They faced backlash over a song they wrote admitting that they were "coming for your children."

The chorus later said the song was simply a parody and they really had no intention of grooming your children for the LGBT lifestyle.

But in reality that's exactly what they are doing. They really are coming.

Disney continues to embrace the LGBT agenda, announcing that a beloved animated series is about to feature a same-sex couple as well as a gender non-conforming character.

Disney announced that Billy Porter from *Kinky Boots* and Zachary Quinto will provide voices for the Disney+ cartoon series.

The Proud Family, which originally aired in the early 2000s, debuted in 2022 as *The Proud Family: Louder and Prouder*.

The two gay dads will be parents to a fourteen-year-old social justice warrior.

"Porter and Quinto voice Randall and Barry Leibowitz Jenkins, adopted parents to 14-year-old activist Maya, played by Keke Palmer. [EJ] Johnson will portray Michael Collins, Penny Proud's best friend guy who is described as a non-conforming trendsetter who serves up fierce looks both at school and on the basketball [*sic*]," Variety reports.[18]

Disney says they have fully embraced the LGBT agenda because they believe in the power of inclusive storytelling.

---

17 Todd Starnes, "'We're Coming for Your Children' - San Francisco Gay Men's Chorus," Todd Starnes, July 7, 2021, https://www.toddstarnes.com/crime/were-coming-for-your-children-san-francisco-gay-mens-chorus/.

18 Haley Bosselman, "'Proud Family' Revival at Disney Plus Adds Billy Porter, Zachary Quinto and EJ Johnson," *Variety*, May 12, 2021, https://variety.com/2021/tv/news/proud-family-disney-plus-billy-porter-zachary-quinto-ej-johnson-1234971592/.

The truth is that Disney has been overrun by radical sex and gender revolutionaries.

This is about indoctrinating small children—and shoving an agenda directly into the faces of American families.

So don't be surprised if the next Disney classic stars a lesbian Snow White and a bunch of transgender dwarfs.

BLUE'S CLUES CELEBRATES GAY PRIDE

Blue's Clues, the popular television program for children, published a Gay Pride video featuring lesbian alligators, transgender beavers, and non-binary dolphins.

Nickelodeon says the sing-along video for kids is part of its celebration of Gay Pride Month.

Nina West, a man who dresses like a woman, provided the voice for the video's animated drag queen.

The cartoon features a parade of LGBT families—like two gay bears, one of whom was wearing a feather boa.

The point is to convince children that families can have two mommies or two daddies, or they can be asexual, bisexual, or pansexual.

"All families are made differently and they love each other so proudly," West warbles. "Allies to the queer community can love their queer friends so proudly. Love is love is love, you see, and everyone should love proudly."

Pansexuality, by the way, has nothing to do with pots, pans, or any other kitchen utensils.

The producer of the cartoon said it was a career highlight to create a pro-gay video for preschoolers.

The folks who originally created *Blue's Clues* said the show was about helping to challenge and build the self-esteem of three-year-olds, not confuse them.

Clearly, when it comes to the traditional family—Nickelodeon doesn't have a clue.

GAY ACTIVIST INVITES KIDS TO CALL HER "AUNTIE"

There is a war raging right now in classrooms all across this nation for the hearts and minds of our children—and right now, the sex and gender revolutionaries are winning that war without even firing a shot.

Stacy Phillips is the mayor pro tempore of Huntersville, North Carolina. She is also a radical pro-gay activist.

The other day Ms. Phillips posted a disturbing message on her Twitter account. She invited children who may be struggling with LGBT issues to reach out to her privately. She said she would be proud to be their "Auntie."

It's creepy—the sort of behavior one would expect from a predator or a pedophile. But it's the latest in a disturbing trend of LGBT activists putting themselves between parents and their kids.

Notices were posted the other day at Eau Claire North High School inviting kids dealing with gender issues to ignore their parents.

"If your parents aren't accepting of your identity, I'm your mom now." That's the message one teacher shared with students. Hashtag: #freemomhugs.

IDAHO KIDS GIVEN LESSON IN INTERCOURSE

Eighth graders at a local middle school in Moscow, Idaho, got a lesson that surely caused their eyes to bug out: a series of lessons about how to have intercourse—graphic lessons. Stuff we are not allowed to even talk about on the radio.

The Idaho Freedom Foundation first exposed the pornographic lessons:[19]

> "Keep the condom on until you ejaculate," says a female narrator. The video switches to a bird exiting a cuckoo clock on the bedroom wall. Trojan's video[20] then shows a hand pushing a used condom up off a shaft. "Immediately after ejaculation, hold the condom in place and withdraw the penis while it is still erect," the narrator says. "Dispose of the used condom by wrapping it in tissue," the narrator adds alongside a depiction of just that.
>
> Titled "Condom Sense," the video was created by Trojan Condoms and shows multiple scenes in which either a bed or car is rocking back and forth in an obvious attempt to depict sexual activity.
>
> Another scene shows the man and woman, whose breast size seems purposefully enhanced, at a table

---

19 Anna Miller and Scott Yenor, "Eighth Grade Students Shown Condom Video with Simulated Sex in Planned Parenthood Endorsed Program," Idaho Freedom Foundation, January 17, 2023, https://idahofreedom.org/eighth-grade-students-shown-condom-video-with-simulated-sex-in-planned-parenthood-endorsed-program/.

20 trojanbrandcondoms, "Trojan Condoms How to Use a Condom," YouTube, March 15, 2012, https://www.youtube.com/watch?v=NBt4BviTZAo.

> where the waiter offers a platter of various types of condoms. "Some have unique shapes, ribbing, nubs – all designed to enhance the experience," the narrator says. NCHD has said that video was shown virtually and in-person at Moscow Middle School from 2019-2020. It was similarly shown in-person at Tammany Alternative School from 2018-2020. Another Trojan video was shown at Moscow Middle School from 2019-2022 and Tammany from 2018-2020. This one outlines, along with footage, how the company manufactures its condoms.
>
> A separate video discusses the history of condoms and includes clips of topless women. That content was revealed as part of a 2018 email in which NCHD Health Education Specialist Jennifer Andrews laid out multiple videos she intended to show students during a presentation for Reducing the Risk (RTR). NCHD says that particular video—dubbed "The History of Condoms"—was utilized at Tammany Alternative School but hasn't been shown since 2018.

The videos were part of a sex education program endorsed by Planned Parenthood and implemented in public schools by the Idaho Department of Health and Welfare.

What's even more disturbing is that parents and taxpayers had to file a records request to get the information—as if the district was making moms and dads go through hoops to find out what their kids had been exposed to.

Call your local public schools. Ask if they are using any Planned Parenthood propaganda in their classrooms. And if they are, you need to mobilize your friends and attend the next school board meeting.

CLASS LESSON INCLUDES MASSAGE OIL AND FEATHER BOAS

Parents in Eugene, Oregon, raised concerns about a shocking homework assignment from Churchill High School.

Their children were instructed to write a short story depicting a sexual fantasy involving feather boas, romantic music, massage oil, and flavored syrup.

"My daughter was very, very, very uncomfortable in the classroom," dad Justin McCall told television station KEZI.[21] "Especially when [the teacher] put up the generated spinning wheel, and it had anal penetration and oral sex up there. Her and her best friend did not participate in that. But they still got graded."

It's not the first time that students had been exposed to inappropriate lessons. Earlier in the school year they had to write the initials of classmates they would consider having sex with.

OregonLive reports the teacher, Kirk Miller, assigned kids a lesson titled, "With Whom Would You Do It."[22]

---

21 Joey Vacca, "More Controversial Assignments in Churchill High School's Health Class Cause Increased Outrage," KEZI 9 News, March 13, 2023, https://www.kezi.com/news/more-controversial-assignments-in-churchill-high-schools-health-class-cause-increased-outrage/article_f6225688-c20b-11ed-b52d-cf59f8c30c59.html?utm_source=substack&utm_medium=email.

22 Julia Silverman, "Eugene Parents Decry High School 'sexual Fantasy' Health Assignment," The Oregonian/OregonLive, March 10, 2023, https://www.oregonlive.com/education/2023/03/eugene-parents-decry-high-school-sexual-fantasy-health-assignment.html.

Parent Katherine Rogers told the newspaper the assignment was to: "List on the handout the initials of a male or a female that you would do each activity with. You may use the same person for multiple activities."

"What are we promoting?" Rogers asked. "What is an adult doing with this information?"

"The district reviews these curriculums before they get approved, right?" she asked. "Did they actually read this? If this was reviewed, how did it slip through the cracks? I could see this easily becoming a national scandal."

The school district says the perverted lesson was part of approved curriculum, but it has since been pulled from the classroom.

That's all well and good, but the issue is who put it there in the first place? And why is that person still employed with the district? And why hasn't the teacher been charged with crimes regarding the distribution of sexually explicit material to minors?

All that to say if your kid's homework assignment involves a tub of Crisco, Barry White music, and a bottle of Mrs. Butterworth's—you might want to consider homeschooling.

5

ATHEISTS DROPKICK CHRISTIANS THROUGH GOALPOSTS

THERE ARE TWO beloved traditions in the Deep South: Friday night football and Sunday morning church.

God and the gridiron are the official religions of the South.

How can we forget that great inspirational song, "Dropkick Me Jesus (Through the Goalposts of Life)"?

And it's not uncommon to hear a preacher deliver an invocation from the memorial press box just before the marching band delivers a rip-roaring rendition of the national anthem.

They've been following that sacred playbook for decades in Jefferson County, Alabama.

But not anymore.

The Freedom From Religion Foundation, a Wisconsin-based group of atheists, agnostics, and free-thinkers, filed a complaint on behalf of a "concerned parent."

It seems as though a godless heathen took offense by prayers delivered before the start of football games at two local high schools.

"Our complainant reports that their child has been made to feel uncomfortable because they don't share the same religious beliefs as most of the other students at their school," read their complaint letter.

The Freedom From Religion Foundation says the Supreme Court has ruled that any invocation delivered over a public address system is unconstitutional—including prayers delivered by students.

"There are people affected by this. I think some people treat it as, oh they just don't want to hear prayer. They don't like that Christians exist. It has nothing to do with that. It truly is just that public schools are a neutral place. They should be neutral with regard to religion," attorney Chris Line told television station WBRC.[1]

The out-of-town atheists said Christian prayers recited over a public address system are illegal.

I find it quite ironic that it's perfectly legal in the United States to burn our flag, to spit on our flag, and to even take a knee during the national anthem (just google Colin Kaepernick).

For many years, it was permissible for a football player to take a knee to protest the flag, but it was illegal for football coaches to take a knee to pray. Of course, all of that changed when the Supreme Court ruled in favor of Joe Kennedy, the Washington State football coach who was fired for praying at the fifty-yard line after high school games. After a lengthy court battle, the

1 Josh Gauntt, "FFRF: Some Jefferson County Schools Ending Prayer over PA System at High School Football Games," 6 WBRC, April 6, 2022, https://www.wbrc.com/2022/04/06/ffrf-some-jefferson-county-schools-ending-prayer-over-pa-system-high-school-football-games/.

coach was awarded millions of dollars in damages, and he got his job back.

The school board's response reminded me of a story I covered from Putnam County, Tennessee. Football coaches at two high schools were targeted by Americans United for Separation of Church and State. It's a radical, left-wing group that wants to remove God from the public marketplace.

They were angered to learn that the coaches had joined football players on the field for post-game prayers.

The school district issued a speedy response: the coaches would no longer be able to pray.

"Courts have consistently ruled that prayer and proselytizing cannot be sponsored by schools or school personnel," the district said in a statement.

The coaches were simply showing solidarity with their young players by offering thanks after a football game. It wasn't a Billy Graham crusade.

Americans United called it a "great win" for separation of church and state (although there is nothing in the Constitution advocating for such a ban).

The sad reality is that in the United States of America, a football coach is allowed to take a knee to protest the flag, but he cannot take a knee to pray to Almighty God.

But the football team would not be bullied by the out-of-town agitators. The following Friday, under the stadium lights, the teenage boys gathered on the field after the game and, on bended knee, did what their coaches could not.

Bob Vick, an alumnus of the Putnam High School, posted a viral image of the moment the students gathered to pray on Facebook.

"Satan's power was defeated tonight, as the threat of legal action to forbid prayer after the game was overwhelmed by player led prayer," Vick wrote. "God bless the Baxter and Stone players for their faith and courage."[2]

Satan's power was indeed defeated at that football game. Neither the gates of Hell nor Americans United will prevail against us.

Anyway, back to Alabama where the school board consulted with their attorneys and decided it would be best to stop the prayers.

"The superintendent met with school principals and the administration will not allow prayer at school-sponsored events, including football games," read a letter from the district's attorney to the out-of-town atheists.

Cowards, all.

A few days later, the superintendent, no doubt feeling the heat from the good church-going football fans, issued another statement saying that fans were still allowed to voluntarily pray—just not over the taxpayer-funded public address system.

"Any assertion that the Jefferson County school system will no longer permit school prayer during school activities is simply not correct," Walter Gonsoulin Jr. wrote in a lengthy letter published by AL.com.[3] "The right to pray and to religious expression is guaranteed under our laws and Constitution. The

---

2 Kaylin Jorge, "Football Players Lead Prayer with Parents, Fans after Game in Putnam County," ABC 15 News, September 20, 2021, https://wpde.com/news/nation-world/football-players-lead-prayer-with-parents-fans-after-game-in-putnam-county.

3 Greg Garrison, "Jefferson County Superintendent Reaffirms 'Voluntary' School Prayer," AL.com, June 27, 2022, https://www.al.com/news/2022/04/jefferson-county-superintendent-reaffirms-voluntary-school-prayer.html.

Superintendent and the Jefferson County Board not only respect those rights, but will do everything in their power to make sure that those rights are protected, respected, and honored."

The superintendent continued, "Our country was founded on these inalienable rights. Our school board and superintendent believe in them. To the extent those rights are attacked or called into question by others who do not live here, who do not have the same respect for those freedoms, and who do not represent the values of our community, this Superintendent and Board will stand with our students, families, employees, and communities in defense of the right to pray and to express their religious beliefs."

There's just one problem with the superintendent's robust defense of religious liberty. Instead of standing with the students, families, employees, and communities in defense of the right to pray and to express religious beliefs, he surrendered the microphone to the squawking out-of-town atheists.

Nevertheless, I doubt this is the last we will be hearing from the good people of Jefferson County. It is Alabama, after all. And I suspect that the school board and the atheists are in for a rude awakening come football season.

Because anybody who's been to a Baptist church revival meeting knows that a hellfire and brimstone preacher does not need a taxpayer-funded public address system to convey his message.

The Good Lord will take care of the amplification.

My uncle Jerry, a good church-going Methodist, was none too happy when I told him about the predicament facing the good people of Alabama.

"It's just too bad we can't dropkick the atheists through the goalposts instead," he told me.

I explained that the Good Book says we have to extend the right hand of Christian fellowship—even to atheists. We have to turn the other cheek.

"What about extending the right boot up their butt cheeks instead?" he asked.

6

Y'ALL, WE NEED TO TALK ABOUT CHICK-FIL-A AND CRACKER BARREL

CHICK-FIL-A IS TESTING a new plant-based entree—a slab of breaded cauliflower tucked between two hot buttered buns and garnished with two pickles.

It's called the "Chick-fil-A Cauliflower Sandwich."

If y'all need to stop reading and grab a comfort bag, I completely understand.

Chick-fil-A says their fake meat sandwich is the perfect centerpiece for their all-new plant-forward menu.

They plan to test this culinary heresy in Denver and the Carolinas. I have no doubt the folks who live in the Mile High City will love the new sandwich. Those folks are so high they'd eat a deep-fried flip flop.

"Cauliflower is the hero of our new sandwich, and it was inspired by our original Chick-fil-A Chicken Sandwich," a company spokesperson said.

The sandwich is apparently so bad that the Chick-fil-A cows are picketing some stores with signs that read, "Eat Sumwhere Else." Well, that's just an unconfirmed rumor.

"Guests told us they wanted to add more vegetables into their diets, and they wanted a plant-forward entrée that tasted uniquely Chick-fil-A. Our new sandwich is made with the highest quality ingredients and whole vegetables, and we hope it offers customers another reason to dine at Chick-fil-A," the spokesperson said.[1]

Well, that's why Chick-fil-A has a side salad on the menu. If they really want more veggies, bring back coleslaw and carrot salad.

Burger King had its "Beyond Burger," and White Castle served up something called an "Impossible Slider." Kentucky Fried Chicken tested plant-based chicken nuggets, but they never made it to the menu. And McDonald's concocted something called a "McPlant sandwich" that was flat-out McNasty.

And then there's the sad situation at Cracker Barrel.

The restaurant chain with the rocking chairs on the front porch rolled out a new item on the menu—something called "Impossible Sausage" made from plants.

"Discover new meat frontiers," the restaurant chain wrote on its Facebook page. "Experience the out of this world flavor of Impossible Sausage Made From Plants."

Nothing says homestyle breakfast like scrambled eggs and sausage made from azalea bushes and ferns.

Cracker Barrel says customers are craving a nutritious plant-based option.

---

1 "Chick-Fil-A Welcomes Cauliflower to the Menu," Chick-fil-A, February 9, 2023, https://www.chick-fil-a.com/stories/news/chick-fil-a-welcomes-cauliflower-to-the-menu#:~:text=%E2%80%9CGuests%20told%20us%20they%20wanted,Chick%2Dfil%2DA.%E2%80%9D.

"At Cracker Barrel, our all-day, homestyle breakfast menu is a staple that draws enthusiasm from guests of all ages, so we are always exploring opportunities to improve how our guests experience breakfast," Cracker Barrel's Sarah Breymaier told Vegconomist.com.[2]

"Our new breakfast menu innovations provide a personalized experience with delicious breakfast choices to satisfy every taste bud—whether guests are nostalgic for homestyle food, hungry for a nutritious plant-based option or have a craving for a sweet treat. At morning, noon or night, we want guests to enjoy crave-able breakfast favorites at a compelling value," she added.

But my social media feed suggests that the fried chicken crowd is not ready to take the plunge.

Folks were riled up. They said the fake meat goes against Cracker Barrel's brand—a brand built on fried chicken and sweet tea, not avocado toast and wheatgrass.

Comfort food, not health food.

And I'm fairly certain the average Cracker Barrel customer is not going to sit down for a plate of vegan biscuits with a side of almond milk gravy.

By the way—there's a reason why they call fake-meat sausage "Impossible." It tastes like wet cardboard harvested from an Antifa homeless encampment.

There's another reason plant-based grub is called "Impossible"—it's impossible to swallow. During my missionary years in Brooklyn, I tried eating one of those fake meat sand-

2 "Cracker Barrel Debuts Impossible Sausage as First Plant-Based Meat Option," Vegconomist, June 21, 2022, https://vegconomist.com/gastronomy-food-service/cracker-barrel-impossible-sausage-option/.

wiches. It went down and came right back up. What I thought was a pickle landed on some poor fellow's man bun.

But let's be honest—if your daily diet includes shots of wheatgrass and organic soy, there's a good chance you're not going to be dining at Chick-fil-A.

What a sad state of affairs at one of our most cherished culinary institutions.

First, they got rid of their chicken salad sandwich. Then, they tossed out the coleslaw and carrot salad. And now, they're desecrating their sacred restaurants with fake poultry.

The phones lit up on my radio show, and many callers, not to mention most of the Starnes family, were concerned that Chick-fil-A had flown the coop.

My sweet great aunt Gardenia-Rose (her mother was a florist) called me in a state of fright.

"Todd, you need to call President Trump right now," she demanded. "He's got to know about this. Everything has done gone catawampus."

"Know about what?" I asked.

"I was at the ladies' Tuesday morning Bible study over in Bucksnort, and Linda Sue Ledbetter—you remember Linda Sue—her boy Tommy John came out as a potted plant, moved to Asheville, and joined a drum circle?"

How could I forget?

"He's dating an azalea bush," she said. "But keep that to yourself. It was an unspoken prayer request."

"So what does this have to do with President Trump?" I asked, trying to get the conversation back on track.

"Well, Linda Sue says that Chick-fil-A may be the anti-Christ," she said in hushed tones.

The anti-Christ? That's ridiculous. Who told her that?

"Her nephew Carl Junior works the brisket station down at the Buc-ee's off Interstate Forty. He does numerology on the side, and according to his cyphers, if you take the number of Chick-fil-A franchises, subtract the number of cauliflower farms in the United States, and divide by the four horsemen, you get [now in a terrified weeping whisper] six-six-six."

I happened to know Carl Jr., no relation to the hamburger chain, and I'd trust Jethro Bodine from *The Beverly Hillbillies* with my accounting before I'd let Carl anywhere near a calculator.

"I need a priest," Aunt Gardenia-Rose declared.

"But you're a Baptist," I interjected.

"It was Preacher Lugnut's idea," she said. "We had Chick-fil-A nuggets at Bible study. I'm so ashamed. I've been possessed by Satan chicken. I need an exorcism."

I assured Aunt Gardenia-Rose that it was highly unlikely the anti-Christ was either pressure cooked in refined peanut oil or covered in feathers. And that uneasiness was probably just a bad case of indigestion.

That being said, I recommended she take a few swigs of Pepto-Bismol and switch to Bojangles. Their fried chicken is deep-fried, and there's no cauliflower on the menu—just like God intended.

7
I MISS AUNT JEMIMA

"I don't want a Black History Month. Black history is American history."

—Hollywood star Morgan Freeman[1]

I'M WRITING THIS chapter inside a tanning booth listening to the theme song from *Shack*. I'm trying to bronze my skin so that I might be eligible for reparations. I've also petitioned to change my name to LeBron Starnes. I figure if other folks can self-identity as black, so can I.

And I'm more than willing to risk skin cancer for a $5 million payout from a city that never even legalized slavery.

The fifteen-member San Francisco African American Reparations Advisory Committee released its hefty recommendation in January as part of a sixty-page report that also includes debt forgiveness.

"Provide a one-time, lump sum payment of $5 million to each eligible person," the report reads.

1 Adam Howard, "The Black History Month Debate Is Back," NBC News, January 22, 2016, https://www.nbcnews.com/news/nbcblk/black-history-month-debate-back-n502226.

"A lump sum payment would compensate the affected population for the decades of harms that they have experienced and will redress the economic and opportunity losses that Black San Franciscans have endured, collectively, as the result of both intentional decisions and unintended harms perpetuated by City policy," it added.

Eric McDonnell, the committee's chair, said it wasn't even something they calculated.

"There wasn't a math formula," McDonnell told the *Washington Post*. "It was a journey for the committee towards what could represent a significant enough investment in families to put them on this path to economic well-being, growth and vitality that chattel slavery and all the policies that flowed from it destroyed."[2]

To be eligible for reparations, an applicant must be at least eighteen years old, "an individual who has identified as 'Black/African American' on public documents for at least 10 years."

But that criteria won't stop me from applying. I'm going to retroactively self-identify as a black person. That, and I can recite the scripts of all the Madea movies from memory.

Now, "LeBron Starnes" might seem like the most ludicrous and laughable joke in this book. But what the professional race agitators have done to our country is no laughing matter. They are advancing radical ideologies that will only lead to the destruction of America and the nuclear family.

---

2 Anders Hagstrom, "San Francisco Reparations Panel on How It Decided on $5m per Black Person: 'There Wasn't a Math Formula,'" Fox News, February 28, 2023, https://www.foxnews.com/politics/san-francisco-reparations-panel-decided-5m-per-black-person-wasnt-math-formula.

That's the literal goal of Black Lives Matter: to destroy traditional American families. And the Left knows that our country's Achilles' heel is race.

Consider what happened in Springfield, Ohio.

A group of black children at Kenwood Elementary School ordered white children to get down on their knees and say, "Black Lives Matter."

Those students who refused to obey were dragged onto the playground and beaten.

One white child was punched in the head. And it was all captured on video.

"They basically told him to get down on his knees and say 'BLM' and if he didn't that they was going to beat him up and all that," Ryan Springer told television station WHIO.[3] Springer's twelve-year-old boy was one of those who was targeted.

The Springfield Police Department confirms that a number of children were assaulted.

Mom Krystal Harr told the *New York Post* her twelve-year-old sixth-grader was among those "forced on his knees Friday and [forced] to say BLM."[4]

She said her son was "terrified."

Denise Williams, the local NAACP president, says the attackers should be held accountable—but should not be arrested.

---

3 WHIO Staff, "Police Pursuing Charges for Students in Racial Incident at Springfield Elementary School," WHIO TV 7, February 20, 2023, https://www.whio.com/news/local/police-give-update-racial-incident-involving-students-springfield-elementary-school/KQB3B3XWPBDVDGQ5IG4NBQRBBQ/.

4 Lee Brown, "Shocking Video Shows Black Kids Attack, Force White Kids to Say 'Black Lives Matter' at Ohio School: Cops," *New York Post*, March 3, 2023, https://nypost.com/2023/03/03/black-kids-forced-white-kids-to-say-black-lives-matter-cops/.

"This is a teachable moment. We need to really educate the school, and the parents," Williams told *Dayton 24/7 Now*.[5]

I completely agree. It is indeed a teachable moment. We need to teach the nation that racism is wrong no matter the skin color.

But not only should the children be arrested—they should all face federal hate crime charges.

This is what critical race theory looks like in practice. It is ugly, it is violent, and it is dangerous.

And let's get real—had white kids been dragging black kids through the playground, the NAACP would've been marching on the school board office demanding jail time.

And we all know that CNN, MSNBC, the *New York Times*, and every other major news outlet would've made it breaking news.

But I doubt any of us are surprised that the racist attack on the white school children in Ohio did not make the national news. That's what happens when all lives don't matter.

In the spring of 2023, downtown Chicago was ground zero for the CRT mobs. Motorists were injured. Stores were looted. Cars destroyed.

"In no way do I condone the destructive activity we saw in the Loop and lakefront this weekend. It is unacceptable and has no place in our city," then mayor-elect Brandon Johnson said in a statement. "However, it is not constructive to demonize youth

---

5 Gwyneth Falloon, "Local NAACP Reacts to What Police Say Is a 'Racially-Motivated' Altercation," Dayton 24/7 Now, February 24, 2023, https://dayton247now.com/news/crisis-in-the-classroom/local-naacp-gets-involved-in-what-police-say-is-a-racially-motivated-altercation.

who have otherwise been starved of opportunities in their own communities."[6]

So the progressive mayor-elect is more concerned that you might demonize the mob that assaulted an innocent young lady or looted a small business owner's store.

Violence was so bad in places like Philadelphia and Memphis that many businesses are shutting down and residents are moving out.

Four Walmart stores are closing in Chicago.

Walmart also announced they were pulling out of war-torn Portland, Oregon. Nike shut down one of its stores over high crime. And Cracker Barrel said they had had enough.

The woke outdoor company REI announced it was shutting down its flagship store in downtown Portland.

In an emailed announcement, they said that the store "had its highest number of break-ins and thefts in two decades, despite actions to provide extra security."

"The extra security measures required to keep customers and employees safe are not financially sustainable," a company spokesperson told OregonLive.[7]

The one common denominator: the mobs are mostly made up of young and angry black teenagers.

This, ladies and gentlemen, is what critical race theory looks like in real life: A generation of children raised to believe they

---

6 NBC 5 Staff, "Mayor-Elect Johnson Addresses Statement on Downtown Disturbances Following Speech in Springfield," NBC 5 Chicago, April 19, 2023, https://www.nbcchicago.com/news/local/mayor-elect-johnson-addresses-statement-on-downtown-disturbances-following-speech-in-springfield/3123003/#:~:text=%22It%20is%20unacceptable%20and%20has,to%20gather%20safely%20and%20responsibly.%22.

7 Kristine de Leon, "REI to Close Only Portland Store, Citing Break-Ins, Theft," The Oregonian/OregonLive, April 17, 2023, https://www.oregonlive.com/business/2023/04/rei-to-close-its-only-portland-store-citing-break-ins-theft.html.

are the oppressed and big business is the oppressor. A generation raised to believe that the police are the enemy. A generation raised to judge white people by the color of their skin.

But it's also about the breakdown of the American family: Parents who are not raising their children with a firm but loving hand. Parents who are allowing their kids to roam the streets well after dark. Parents who are not teaching their kids right from wrong.

It's past time to get your kids off the streets and into a church, and out of the public schools and into a private or homeschool. That's the only way to fix what is broken in America.

CONFEDERATE STATUE REPLACED WITH GIANT AFRO-PICK

From Memphis comes word that a statue of Jefferson Davis, the former president of the Confederacy, has been replaced with a giant afro-pick and black power fist.

The eight-foot-tall afro-pick and black power fist are part of a temporary art installation in Fourth Bluff Park, previously known as Confederate Park.

In 2018, the park underwent a cultural cleansing. Every Civil War statue, sign, and plaque was removed.

"You know, change is never easy," Greenspace CEO Van Turner told Action News 5. "But change is necessary."

The new art installation is titled, "All Power to All People." But clearly, they don't mean "all" people.

"This is a celebration of self-love, representation and something that we can all really be proud of," George Abbott with Memphis River Parks told the television station.[8]

---

8 Jacob Gallant, "'All Power to All People' Art Piece Comes to Fourth Bluff Park," Action News 5, April 3, 2023, https://www.actionnews5.com/2023/04/04/all-power-all-people-art-piece-comes-fourth-bluff-park/.

Action News 5 reports that "while one might see an afro pick with a power fist, others might have a different take."

How in the world people might have a different interpretation of the art installation is beyond me. It's literally an afro-pick and a giant black power fist.

"Bringing all power to all people here just helps to emphasize what we try to do every day which is create a riverfront for everyone," Abbott said. "I think it's a beautiful piece in and of itself. But the meaning behind it adds a layer of meaning that's very profound here in Memphis."

In Memphis, city leaders are literally renaming all parks and buildings named after white people. They are also tearing down statues and monuments honoring whites. They even tried to rename Poplar Avenue, a major commercial thoroughfare, in honor of Black Lives Matter. Who knew that trees were racist?

Several years back, city leaders even dug up the dead bodies of a Confederate war general and his wife. They literally desecrated the grave of Nathan Bedford Forrest because it was in a public park that had been previously named in his honor.

Maybe instead of calling it Fourth Bluff Park, the city council should rename it "Afro-Pick Park."

KIDS TRIGGERED BY CHICKEN AND WAFFLES

Big trouble at Nyack Middle School in New York.

The cafeteria served chicken and waffles to kick off Black History Month. The children were also given a watermelon-themed dessert.

The principal said he was horrified and apologized for the cultural insensitivity displayed by their food provider.

Principal David Johnson went on to say that the menu reflected negative stereotypes concerning the African-American community.

"We are extremely disappointed by this regrettable situation and apologize to the entire Nyack community," the principal said in a statement. "I am disappointed that Aramark would serve items that differed from the published monthly menu. Especially items that reinforce negative stereotypes concerning the African-American Community."[9]

Aramark said the timing of the menu was unfortunate, and the lunch ladies were supposed to serve something else.

"While our menu was not intended as a cultural meal, we acknowledge that the timing was inappropriate, and our team should have been more thoughtful in its service," the Aramark statement said. "This was a mistake and does not represent the values of our company, and we are committed to doing better in the future."

Gotta say I'm sure the kids would rather feast on chicken and waffles instead of mystery meat and a vegetable medley.

So, now the lunch ladies are heading to cultural sensitivity class.

Yet no one has been able to explain exactly why that particular menu is racially offensive. I know plenty of white folks who love eating chicken. We call it the Gospel Bird back home in Tennessee.

Not racist—just finger-licking good.

---

9 "Vendor Apologizes for School Lunch Served on 1st Day of Black History Month," ABC7 New York, February 3, 2023, https://abc7ny.com/nyack-aramark-school-lunch-controversy/12766946/.

Who knew that chicken and waffles would trigger such a massive case of indigestion among the perpetually offended Generation Z crowd?

Thank goodness the lunch ladies didn't serve Mrs. Butterworth's.

COTTON LESSON LANDS TEACHER IN HOT WATER

A teacher at San Francisco's Creative Arts Charter School wanted her eighth grade students to understand the hardships of slavery.

She was teaching a lesson about the invention of the cotton gin.

So she brought cotton plants to class so the kids could feel the sharp edges—so they could see how difficult it was to pull out the seeds.

Some twenty-four hours later, the teacher was removed from the classroom for five weeks, and the school district apologized, calling the lesson unacceptable. They said the teacher violated the school's anti-racist, progressive curriculum.

Putting raw cotton in the hands of children recreates conditions that "evoke so many deeply hurtful things about this country," the mother of a biracial student told the *San Francisco Chronicle*.[10]

"There are people who think this lesson plan promotes empathy; I've heard that and understand that," she said. "There are a lot of people who don't understand why it's hurtful or offensive."

Another parent told the newspaper it was unbearably cruel how they treated one of the most beloved teachers at the school.

10 Jill Tucker, "S.F. Teacher Used a Cotton Plant to Teach about Slavery. The Fallout Has Divided Parents," *San Francisco Chronicle*, April 22, 2022, https://www.sfchronicle.com/bayarea/article/An-S-F-teacher-used-a-cotton-plant-to-teach-17121022.php.

"I think it's insane they would treat a teacher like this and basically discard a teacher that has been so inspiring and dedicated," said the parent. "It feels like it was a lesson in sensitivity and empathy. That's why my mind is so blown and I can't stop being angry about it."

The teacher was allowed to return to the classroom five weeks later—armed with a personal apology.

"Prior to spring break, I taught a tactile lesson involving raw cotton in an effort to get the students to understand the difficulty of manually processing cotton prior to the invention of Eli Whitney's Cotton Gin," she wrote in the letter obtained by the *Chronicle*. "While this lesson was sourced from reliable sources, after conferring with the administration and hearing many of the student's reflections, I realize that this lesson was not culturally responsive and had the potential to cause harm."

I wonder how many of the aggrieved parents and students actually wear clothing made from cotton? The commercial tells us that cotton is the fabric of our lives—but now it's apparently racist.

Might want to switch to polyester, America.

USC SAYS "FIELD" IS RACIST

Let's say you are at a social gathering, and someone asks, "What sort of work you do?" You might tell them that you are a scientist, and your field of study is genetics.

But that would be a big cultural no-no at the University of Southern California. The School of Social Work there is telling people to avoid the word "field."

"Specifically, we have decided to remove the term 'field' from our curriculum and practice and replace it with 'practicum,'" read a letter from the university obtained by Fox News. "This change supports anti-racist work practice by replacing language that would be considered anti-Black or anti-immigrant in favor of inclusive language."[11]

I suspect it won't be long before they ban fried chicken from the dining hall, and soon students will no longer be allowed to wear clothing made of cotton.

"Language can be powerful, and phrases such as 'going into the field' or 'field work' maybe have connotations for descendants of slavery and immigrant workers that are not benign," the letter continued.

So, what are they going to call that great big patch of grass that the Trojans play football on every Saturday?

BLACK LAWMAKER TRIGGERED BY WHITE SKIN

Shelby County, Tennessee, Commissioner Britney Thornton, a progressive Democrat, said she was triggered by a white Republican commissioner's whiteness.

"I own the fact that today your whiteness triggered me because it is actually an identity that I recognize postures you differently from me," the black commissioner said during a contentious commission meeting. "It comes from privileges that I simply do not have."[12]

---

11 Kendall Tietz, "California University Office Will No Longer Use the Word 'Field' Over Racist 'Connotations,'" Fox News, January 11, 2023, https://www.foxnews.com/media/california-university-longer-word-field-over-racist-connotations.

12 Todd Starnes, "Commissioner Britney Thornton: 'Your Whiteness Triggered Me,'" KWAM, February 23, 2023, https://mighty990.com/commissioner-britney-thornton-your-whiteness-triggered-me/.

Her jaw-dropping, racist comments came during a debate over whether to spend $5 million in taxpayer money to fund a study that would provide reparations to black citizens of the county.

"The conversation at hand, though, it's steeped in racial identity. There are just some basic social justice elements to it that we should all be sensitive to," Thornton said.

The commission, which is controlled by black Democrats, overwhelmingly approved the measure. It's unclear if the commission will use only money from white taxpayers to fund the study.

"Today has been a really polarized day. Though some of us in our delegation have never lived a single day as a black person…that that should prohibit you from being able to see a clear opportunity to right some ills," she said.

Thornton said she was triggered by Commissioner Amber Mills, a Republican who lives in the Memphis suburbs.

"I tried to have a conversation with a fellow commissioner and she felt a little triggered by my whiteness," Mills said. "That's where we are these days. And now we are doing resolutions where certain people get reparations."

Mills, who was one of three Republicans to vote against the measure, said she was stunned by outrage over her comments.

"It's come to a point where our skin color—you can't even have a conversation with people," she said. "All this is doing is dividing a community in a desperate time when we really need to unite."

But the purpose of reparations is not to unite, it's meant to divide. It's about taking money from one ethnicity and giving it to another. It's unconstitutional and it's immoral.

"If I'm triggered, it is what it is," Thornton said.

PARENTS FORCED TO SIGN ANTI-RACIST STATEMENT

Brearley School, a female-only prep school located in Manhattan's Upper East Side, requires parents to attend two "diversity, equity, inclusion and anti-racism (DEIA) workshops per school year," according to an admissions application.

Further, prospective parents must write a five-hundred-word essay outlining their commitment to diversity, equity, and inclusion.

Once the students are admitted, parents have to sign an "anti-racist" statement affirming they will take part in diversity events and conversations at the school.

The statement reads, "We expect teachers, staff members, students and parents to participate in anti-racist training and to pursue meaningful change through deliberate and measurable actions. These actions include identifying and eliminating policies, practices and beliefs that uphold racial inequality in our community."

Brearley is not the only prestigious NYC school obsessed with the topic of race.

The *New York Post* reports that the Chaplin School holds optional panel discussions for prospective families on the topic of race. "They take attendance, they have name tags, there is someone from the admissions office to keep track of who goes and who doesn't," a parent told the *New York Post.* "If you don't go, your child is not going to go very far in the admission process."[13]

---

13 Jon Levine, "Elite $60K-a-Year NYC Schools Forcing Woke Indoctrination on Parents, Too," *New York Post,* October 22, 2022, https://nypost.com/2022/10/22/elite-nyc-prep-schools-aim-woke-indoctrination-at-parents-too/.

WHITE TENTH GRADERS TOLD THEY ARE RACIST

Parents pushed back after finding out a tenth grade English assignment told their children: "You are racist."

ABC 7 News reports students at Somers High School in Westchester, New York, texted photos of journal prompts from an optional assignment about "white fragility" to their parents.

"Most of them weren't questions, they were statements: you are a racist," mom Sarah Kooluris said to the ABC affiliate.[14]

The controversial prompts on the handout were derived from Layla Saad's book, *Me and White Supremacy*.

The assignment asked the students questions like, "How does your white fragility show up in conversations about race?" and "Have you ever weaponized your fragility against people of color?" per the outlet's report.

Dom DeMartino, another parent in the school district, said he supports classroom discussions on race but called this method a "problem."

"We want DEI, we want Diversity, Equity and Inclusion, but this person and the way the school has gone about things like this is what's causing the problem," DeMartino said.

While many of the parents were not happy about the lesson, some supported it.

Elana Sofko, another mom in the district, said she wants the students to have difficult conversations about race because she says her students have experienced anti-Semitism in the schools.

---

14 Marcus Solis, "Controversy Brewing at Westchester School District over Assignment Based on Book Addressing Racism," ABC7 New York, November 4, 2022, https://abc7ny.com/controversy-race-somers-high-school-english/12417922/.

School district officials responded by telling parents the assignment was not authorized and is contrary to the school's instructional policies.

"We discovered today that a teacher at Somers High School introduced a lesson in 10th grade English classes that included excerpts from the book *Me and White Supremacy* by Layla Saad. The lesson was immediately discontinued, and the excerpts were pulled from use in the classroom. The district was not aware that this particular lesson was being taught, nor that the excerpts were being used. We immediately began an investigation to determine how the text made it into the classroom," an official statement issued by the district read.

It continued, "Somers High School staff will follow up with the students who were in class for this lesson to ensure that they are properly supported. We will also be reminding our faculty of our BOE policy as it relates to curriculum and classroom instruction. We are committed to ensuring that our classrooms are welcoming, balanced environments where all students are able to thrive."

SCHOOL TEACHES FOUR-YEAR-OLDS HOW TO DEAL WITH RACIST FAMILY MEMBERS

A Washington, DC, elementary school gave students ranging from pre-K to third grade a presentation on how to be anti-racists.

On top of teaching the children that white people "hold all of the power in America," the presentation asked the students to identify racism in themselves and their family members.

Danielle Singh, the principal of Janney Elementary School, explained the event to parents in an open letter.

"Today students in grades pre-k through third grade participated in the Anti-Racism Fight Club presentation with Doyin Richards," the principal wrote. "As part of this work, each student has a fist book to help continue the dialogue at school and home."[15]

During the presentation from the "Anti-Racism Fight Club Fistbook for Kids," the "dealing with racist family members" section told students, "Just because someone is older than you doesn't mean that they're right all of the time."[16]

When explaining what racism from family members may look like, Richards presented a scenario where a family member criticizes the Black Lives Matter movement as an example of racism that should be confronted.

Rather than telling the students to seek out truth when it comes to issues of race, the fistbook told the kids to, "Sit back and listen to BIPOC (black, indigenous, and people of color) and then ask questions. Remember, this isn't a time to share your own experiences."

The presentation also told the students that when minorities and people of color are mean to them to dismiss it in the name of anti-racism.

"Some days BIPOC may be mean to you, but keep in mind that it's rarely personal," the children's book reads. "You still need to show up anyway. Remember, being anti-racist requires effort."

---

15 Gina Martinez, "DC Elementary School Told Four-Year-Old Students to Identify Racists within Their Own Family in 'Anti-Racism Fight Club' Presentation," *Daily Mail*, May 3, 2022, https://www.dailymail.co.uk/news/article-10780375/DC-elementary-school-gave-presentation-helped-identify-racists-family.html.

16 Doyin Richards, "ARFC Fistbook for Kids," Anti-Racism Fight Club, 2020, https://drive.google.com/file/d/1XHjFajb8vyzz6W_kQNc_2zfQ8Kuyi_G8/view.

In addition to writing this book for kids, Fox News Digital reports[17] that Doyin Richards,[18] the founder of the Anti-Racism Fight Club, also wrote a fistbook for adults.

"Racism is as American as apple pie and baseball," the book for adults states.

"As we sit here today, it is still woven into the fabric of our homes, communities, schools, government, economic system, healthcare, and so much more. As a matter of fact, it would be difficult to find one facet of our society where racism does not exist. White supremacy isn't the shark, it's the ocean."

COACH FORCED TO APOLOGIZE FOR RECRUITING WHITE QUARTERBACK

Big trouble at Albany State University—one of the nation's historically black colleges.

Football Coach Quinn Gray is under fire after he recruited a white athlete—Marcus Stokes—a four-star high school quarterback.

Turns out the young man was seen on a video singing along to a rap song which included a racially-charged word. One that we will not repeat on the radio or anywhere else for that matter.

Stokes had previously lost a scholarship offer from the University of Florida after the video first went viral.

He offered a sincere apology—and said he accepted the consequences of his behavior.

---

17 Jessica Chasmar and Kelly Laco, "DC Elementary School Gave 4-Year-Olds 'Anti-Racism' 'Fistbook' Asking Them to Identify Racist Family Members," Fox News, May 2, 2022, https://www.foxnews.com/politics/dc-elementary-anti-racism-fistbook-racist-family-members.

18 Doyin Richards, "The Anti-Racism Fight Club," Doyin Richards, October 5, 2022, https://doyinrichards.com/.

"I was in my car listening to rap music, rapping along to the words and posted a video of it on social media," he wrote. "I deeply apologize for the words in the song that I chose to say. It was hurtful and offensive to many people, and I regret that."

"I fully accept the consequences for my actions, and I respect the University of Florida's decision to withdraw my scholarship offer to play football. My intention was never to hurt anybody and I recognize that even when going along with a song, my words still carry a lot of weight. I will strive to be better and to become the best version of myself on and off the field," the teenager went on to say.[19]

Coach Gray wanted to offer the young man a second chance—but he was fiercely rebuked by university officials.

"The president has made it clear that my actions did not meet [ASU's] standard [of excellence]. It was never my intent to misrepresent what ASU stands for nor to ignore the rich history of this institution," he wrote in a statement to Fox News.[20] "My actions caused you to question my commitment to our institution and our ancestors."

Long story short—Albany State rescinded the scholarship offer, and the coach issued a formal apology:

"Let me start with a humble apology. An apology for not honoring the tradition and history of ASU and for letting many of you down," Gray said in his statement. "I didn't uphold the

---

19 Nick Selbe, "Florida QB Recruit Apologizes After Racial Slur Costs Scholarship," *Sports Illustrated*, November 20, 2022, https://www.si.com/college/2022/11/20/florida-quarterback-recruit-apologizes-racial-slur-lost-scholarship.

20 Joe Morgan, "HBCU Coach Apologizes after Offering Scholarship to Student Dropped by Florida for Rapping N-Word," Fox News, January 28, 2023, https://www.foxnews.com/sports/hbcu-coach-apologizes-after-offering-scholarship-student-dropped-florida-rapping-n-word.

Ramily standard that I know you expect. Please know that my decision to speak with a student that did not meet your expectations was unacceptable. I only wanted the best for our team, athletes, and institution when I invited the student to visit ASU. As I say to our players, 'there is a consequence to every action.'

"The consequences of my actions brought pain to our University. I was trying to help a student get back in competition, and in my haste, I did not consider the impact the decision would have on all of you. Frankly, it wasn't my place to use ASU as the platform for redemption in this case. I regret that I used flawed judgment. If given the opportunity, I will do better."

I can't imagine a more cold-hearted and callous institution of higher learning than Albany State University.

A young man made a mistake. He confessed to that mistake. He accepted the consequences of that mistake. And their response was to shun this teenage boy.

I'd be curious to know how the university would respond if a black quarterback had been caught singing along to his favorite rap artist? I suspect we all know the answer to that question.

White parents—I want you to listen very intently to what I'm about to say. You need to find out what sort of music your kids are listening to. Police their playlist and remove any music that includes racially-charged language.

There's a target on their backs for the rest of their lives—because of critical race theory.

PROFESSOR SAYS ALL WHITE PEOPLE ARE RACIST

Marc Lamont Hill, a professor at Temple University and a host on *Black News Tonight*, made a shockingly racist statement during a recent broadcast.

Guest Liz Wheeler asked Hill, point blank, if he thought all white people are inherently racist.

Hill's response was honest and quite frankly, repulsive.

"I don't know if you are backing me into a corner with that question, but yes, I do," he said.

If you are a white student at Temple University you might want to consider dropping Professor Hill's class.

THE DAY THE CULTURE WAR JIHADISTS BEHEADED AUNT JEMIMA

I have sad news to report from the baked goods aisle of your local supermarket. Our beloved Aunt Jemima has been decapitated by the culture jihadists.

Quaker Foods North America announced in 2021 that they were going to rename Aunt Jemima syrup and pancake mix.

I wrote a book about this sort of nonsense called, *Culture Jihad: How to Stop the Left From Killing a Nation.*[21] I would encourage you to buy a copy and read it while eating your syrup-free pancakes.

Quaker Foods said the origin of Aunt Jemima is based on a racial stereotype.

"We recognize Aunt Jemima's origins are based on a racial stereotype," Kristin Kroepfl told NBC News. "As we work to make

21 Todd Starnes, *Culture Jihad: How to Stop the Left from Killing a Nation* (Nashville, TN: Post Hill Press, 2019).

progress toward racial equality through several initiatives, we also must take a hard look at our portfolio of brands and ensure they reflect our values and meet our consumers' expectations."[22]

Culture jihadists, the name I've given to leftists who want to destroy our history, were overjoyed by the news.

"Aunt Jemima is a retrograde image of Black womanhood on store shelves," Cornell University professor Riché Richardson told the TODAY show. "It's an image that harkens back to the antebellum plantation."

She said it's the kind of stereotype that is premised on "this idea of Black inferiority and otherness."

What in the name of Scarlett O'Hara is wrong with these people?

"It is urgent to expunge our public spaces of a lot of these symbols that for some people are triggering and represent terror and abuse," she said.

In the words of Tyler Perry's Madea, the culture jihadists should put the shut to the up.

In recent years, Quaker removed the mammy kerchief from the character. But that was not good enough for the cancel culture mob. Quaker says the only way to make progress toward racial equality is by creating a new non-racist breakfast product.

They also plan to donate $5 million to create engagement in the black community.

The makers of Uncle Ben's Rice went through a similar controversy several years ago. They kept Uncle Ben but made him a wealthy business owner. Instead of Uncle Ben, he's Chairman Ben.

---

22 Ben Kesslen, "Aunt Jemima Brand to Change Name, Remove Image That Quaker Says Is 'Based on a Racial Stereotype,'" NBC News, June 17, 2020, https://www.nbcnews.com/news/us-news/aunt-jemima-brand-will-change-name-remove-image-quaker-says-n1231260.

It's hard to know what's going to trigger the cancel culture next—Oreo Cookies? Duke's Mayonnaise? White Lily Flour?

But when the cancel culture crowd goes after our breakfast food, they've gone too far. What's next? Banning the Irish guy from the Lucky Charms? And heaven help the poor kid who starts his day with a bowl of Cocoa Puffs—or Fruity Pebbles.

If nothing else, the culture jihadists are giving Americans a bad case of indigestion. Seriously, folks.

WHITE FOLKS SING BLACK SPIRITUALS AND ALL HELL BREAKS LOOSE

Should white people sing black spirituals?

Western Michigan University is grappling with that question after a black student was triggered and suffered a social media meltdown when a predominantly white choir sang "Wade in the Water."[23]

"So apparently Western Michigan University thinks it's ok for WHITE peoples to sing negro spirituals while the instructor talking about 'these songs don't belong to one race.' They sure as hell DO," WMU music major Shaylee Faught wrote on a social media post now seen by more than one million people.[24]

Faught got triggered after the choir's black conductor reportedly told the audience that the selections were "American songs" performed "for everyone" and "have no ethnicity."

---

23 Todd Starnes, "White Choir Sings Black Spirituals and All Hell Breaks Loose," The Patriot Post, February 29, 2020, https://patriotpost.us/opinion/68890-white-choir-sings-black-spirituals-and-all-hell-breaks-loose-2020-02-29.

24 Anagha Srikanth, "University Choir Sparks Questions over Who Can Sing Black Spirituals," The Hill, February 24, 2020, https://thehill.com/changing-america/respect/diversity-inclusion/484335-university-choir-sparks-questions-over-who-can/.

The performance, "Spirituals: From Ship to Shore," included songs like "Go Down, Moses" and "Wade in the Water."

Well, faster than you could say "Zip-a-Dee-Doo-Dah," nearly the entire campus suffered a meltdown.

"We as a collective are appalled that this took place on our campus," the Black Student Union (BSU) wrote in a statement. "This act is a further example and reflection of the racial insensitivity and ignorance that has been allowed to occur on Western Michigan's campus."[25]

The BSU called for "racial re-education on sensitivity training and cultural competence."

I have no idea what that means, but it sounds like one of Bernie Sanders's gulags.

University leaders released a statement to WKZO expressing their grave concerns over the matter.[26]

"This student's perspective is real and it is important," they wrote. "It is one among many different perspectives."

John Wesley Wright, who is a renowned conductor and professor, told the Western Herald that he has no idea why the student got triggered, and he has no reason to apologize.[27]

"I just got off the phone with the bass from 'Sweet Honey in The Rock,' (an African-American a cappella ensemble) and her

---

25 Samuel J. Robinson, "WMU School of Music Show Accused of Cultural Appropriation," Western Herald, February 21, 2020, https://www.westernherald.com/community_culture/article_5abf5768-54c2-11ea-9bec-57446ebed23f.html.

26 "Video of WMU Spirituals Choir Concert Sparks Controversy," WKZO, February 21, 2021, https://wkzo.com/2020/02/21/video-of-wmu-spirituals-choir-concert-sparks-controversy/987254/.

27 Samuel J. Robinson, "Viral Video of WMU Choir Sparks Appropriation Debate: WSA Joins BSU in Demand for Apology," Western Herald, February 24, 2020, https://www.westernherald.com/news/article_46b2217c-56c7-11ea-8502-07f9b3df0daf.html.

first question was, 'Has anyone looked into the mental health of the people who made those comments?'" he told the newspaper.

The professor's comment set off the Western Student Association who condemned the "insidious nature of cultural appropriation."

"When the director is more concerned with investigating the mental health of a student rather than empathetically responding to concerns of students, it further illustrates that student's [*sic*] voices do not matter," they wrote in a statement to the newspaper. "We do not and will not tolerate these inappropriate responses."

The snowflakes who run the Black Student Union demanded an apology from the School of Music.

"To decrease the likelihood of events like this happening in the future, we demand that whatever culture, race, or ethnicity is being represented must be consulted before the show," the BSU wrote.[28]

In other words, the choir may want to take a pass on that spring concert medley featuring the works of Dr. Dre and Lil Nasty.

BIRD BRAINED: MEMPHIS WANTS TO RENAME AUDUBON PARK

The Memphis City Council will discuss renaming a beloved and historic city park because someone got triggered by the name.

Council Member Patrice Robinson sponsored two ordinances that were set to be discussed by the council in executive session to rename Audubon Park. The park was named in honor of nineteenth century naturalist John James Audubon.[29]

---

28 Western Michigan BSU (@bsuwmu), "The Black Student Union has seen the incident…" Instagram photo, February 21, 2020, https://www.instagram.com/p/B81yYq8hGGI/?igshid=dvl77hzhqlou.

29 Bill Dries, "Council Member Proposes Name Change for Audubon Park," Daily Memphian, January 23, 2023, https://dailymemphian.com/section/neighborhoods/article/33657/aububon-park-would-become-memphis-botanical-park.

Should Councilwoman Robinson get her way, the park would be renamed in honor of Miriam DeCosta-Willis, a black civil rights activist.

"Removing the name John James Audubon from a prominent culturally-inclusive park is important in communicating a message of diversity, inclusion and unity in Memphis. If the Memphis City Council wishes to name the park, or any public spaces, for an individual, there are Memphians and non-Memphians who are more than deserving of this honor," wrote Thelma Crivens in a column published by the *Daily Memphian.*[30]

Crivens is a member of the notorious City Council Renaming Commission—a collection of culture jihadists who have been tasked with turning the city's past into a heaping pile of rubble.

She noted that Audubon was "a white supremacist and enslaver who bought and sold enslaved people, opposed the abolitionist movement and considered African Americans and Native Americans inferior."

Audubon died in 1851 and was unavailable for comment.

"After growing up as an African American woman in segregated Memphis, I am pleased to see that the city is removing these controversial statues and names," Crivens wrote.

In recent years, the Memphis City Council has taken an aggressive approach to erasing and whitewashing the city's history. They've renamed three parks that had ties to the Civil War—Nathan Bedford Forrest Park, Jefferson Davis Park, and Confederate Park.

---

30 Thelma Crivens, "Opinion: We Must Rename Audubon Park," Daily Memphian, January 18, 2023, https://dailymemphian.com/article/33537/memphis-opinion-rename-audubon-park-john-james-audubon.

And they most recently desecrated the grave of Nathan Bedford Forrest. In Memphis, even the Confederate dead are not allowed to rest in peace.

Quite frankly, the city should just save the taxpayers time and money and rename any building, street, or park that's been named after a dead white guy.

And for that matter, they should also rename the city of Memphis. Anyone who's read the Old Testament knows Egypt has a particularly nasty history when it comes to slavery.

SCARLETT O'HARA HAD A BETTER CHANCE AGAINST THE YANKEES

HBO Max has removed the Oscar-winning Civil War epic *Gone with the Wind* from its library over concerns about racial tensions following the death of George Floyd.

I was ridiculed by many in the conservative and the leftist media for my assertion that we were approaching a day when book banning and movie banning would become the norm in American society.

And producers for several well-known prime-time conservative television hosts refused to promote my book. As I've said many times in the past, most of the people who work in conservative media are not in fact conservatives.

"*Gone with the Wind* is a product of its time and depicts some of the ethnic and racial prejudices that have, unfortunately, been commonplace in American society," HBO said in a statement. "These racist depictions were wrong then and are wrong today, and we felt that to keep this title up without an explanation and a denouncement of those depictions would be irresponsible."

The film won eight Oscars, including best picture, and made history when Hattie McDaniel became the first black American to win an Oscar for her performance.

"These depictions are certainly counter to WarnerMedia's values, so when we return the film to HBO Max, it will return with a discussion of its historical context and a denouncement of those very depictions but will be presented as it was originally created because to do otherwise would be the same as claiming these prejudices never existed. If we are to create a more just, equitable, and inclusive future, we must first acknowledge and understand our history," the HBO statement continued.[31]

John Ridley, who won an Academy Award for *12 Years a Slave*, praised HBO's decision to pull the film.

"It is a film that glorifies the antebellum south. It is a film that, when it is not ignoring the horrors of slavery, pauses only to perpetuate some of the most painful stereotypes of people of color," he wrote.

I wonder if Mr. Ridley would be so bold as to call for the banning of rap and hip hop music that glorifies violence against police officers and women? It's doubtful.

"Let me be real clear: I don't believe in censorship," he wrote. Now that's laughable because that's exactly what he's doing.

"I don't think 'Gone With the Wind' should be relegated to a vault in Burbank. I would just ask, after a respectful amount of time has passed, that the film be re-introduced to the HBO Max platform along with other films that give a more broad-based

31 Julia Alexander, "HBO Max Temporarily Removes Gone with the Wind Because of 'Racist Depictions,'" The Verge, June 10, 2020, https://www.theverge.com/2020/6/10/21286356/hbo-max-gone-with-the-wind-temporarily-removes-racist.

and complete picture of what slavery and the Confederacy truly were," he wrote.

"Or, perhaps it could be paired with conversations about narratives and why it's important to have many voices sharing stories from different perspectives rather than merely those reinforcing the views of the prevailing culture," he added.

As I wrote in *Culture Jihad*, the Left is hell-bent on tearing down statues of Robert E. Lee and Christopher Columbus. They are banning books like *The Adventures of Huckleberry Finn*, *Little House on the Prairie*, and *To Kill a Mockingbird*.[32]

And unless freedom-loving patriots of all races and political parties rise up against these jihadists, we will live the dystopian future predicted in George Orwell's *1984*.

Remember his prophetic words:

> Every record has been destroyed or falsified, every book rewritten, every picture has been repainted, every statue and street building has been renamed, every date has been altered. And the process is continuing day by day and minute by minute. History has stopped.

Our statues are being toppled. Our streets are being renamed. Our books are being rewritten. And our films are being destroyed.

TOO MANY WHITE FOLKS DOING JAZZ HANDS ON BROADWAY

The Great White Way is too White.

That's according to the folks in charge of *The Lion King*.

---

32 Becky Little, "Why 'to Kill a Mockingbird' Keeps Getting Banned," History.com, May 10, 2023, https://www.history.com/news/why-to-kill-a-mockingbird-keeps-getting-banned.

A white sign-language interpreter was fired from his Broadway job because of his skin color.

Keith Wann is one of two white people who were forced off the production by the nonprofit Theatre Development Fund.

That's the organization that staffs Broadway shows with sign language interpreters.

The group decided it was "no longer appropriate to have white interpreters represent black characters for ASL Broadway shows."

Mr. Wann says he was told via email that he was being replaced because of the current social climate.

The *New York Post* obtained additional emails that referenced Lisa Carling, the director of accessibility programs for the Theatre Development Fund. She called for the removal of all non-black interpreters:[33]

> [Lisa] Carling's decision came at the behest of Shelly Guy, the director of ASL for "The Lion King," and called for Carling to get rid of all non-black interpreters, according to another email obtained by The Post and cited in the suit.
>
> "The majority of the characters in the Lion King are black actors and the content takes place in Africa," Guy wrote Carling on April 1.
>
> "Keith Wann, though an amazing ASL performer, is not a black person and therefore should not be representing Lion King," she declared.

33 Jacob Geanous, "White 'Lion King' Sign-Language Interpreter Says He Was Ousted over Skin Color," *New York Post*, November 12, 2022, https://nypost.com/2022/11/12/lion-king-sign-language-interpreter-keith-wann-says-he-was-fired-for-being-white/?utm_source=twitter&utm_campaign=android_nyp.

Mr. Wann has filed a federal lawsuit alleging discrimination. But the decision goes beyond discrimination—it's racism.

Mr. Wann was judged by the color of his skin.

"To me, just seeing that discrimination, it doesn't matter if I'm white or black," Wann told the *Post*. "This is blatant and I would just hope that other people who have also experienced this would step forward."

But if the new rule on Broadway is that actors must reflect the skin color of the characters they are portraying, that spells big trouble for the cast of *Hamilton*.

Our Founding Fathers were a bunch of lily-white straight dudes.

WEARING A SUIT IS RACIST

Dress codes are racist, according to the newest member of the Tennessee House of Representatives.

State Rep. Justin Pearson is a radical black activist from Memphis. And he's facing criticism from his fellow lawmakers over his wardrobe.

The other day, Mr. Pearson showed up on the House floor in a combed-out afro and wearing a black dashiki. The blouse is associated with West African culture.

Mr. Pearson told radio station WPLN that the blouse symbolizes resistance.

"This dress is resistance. This afro is resistance. What we are doing here is subversive to the status quo, and I think that's going to continue to make people uncomfortable," he told the radio station.

Republican lawmaker David Hawk blasted Mr. Pearson, accusing him of violating decorum.

It's been a long-standing practice for men to wear a suit and tie and women to wear formal business attire.

Mr. Hawk recounted the time he was banned from entering the House chamber because he was not wearing a tie.

The person who gave that order was Lois DeBerry—then serving in House leadership—a black woman.

"I showed up one Monday night on two wheels trying to get in here, and I did not have a tie on. And she reminded me that 'Rep. Hawk, if you don't have a tie on, you don't get to walk in that door,'" the lawmaker said.[34]

Mr. Pearson remains defiant and accused his fashion critics of being white supremacists.

"We literally just got on the State House floor and already a white supremacist has attacked my wearing of my Dashiki. Resistance and subversion to the status quo ought to make some people uncomfortable," he wrote on Twitter. "Thank you to every Black Ancestor who made this opportunity possible."

The Tennessee House Republicans said the rules governing decorum and dress were approved with bipartisan support.

"If you don't like rules, perhaps you should explore a different career opportunity," the Republicans wrote on Twitter.

But Mr. Pearson told WPLN that being forced to wear a coat and tie is a form of white supremacy.[35]

"What's happening here is you have discriminatory practices and policies to help homogenize this community to look like

34 Blaise Gainey, "A New Tennessee Lawmaker Walks into the Capitol Wearing a Dashiki. House GOP Suggests He Explore Other Careers.," WPLN News, February 10, 2023, https://wpln.org/post/a-new-tennessee-lawmaker-walks-into-the-capitol-wearing-a-dashiki-house-gop-suggests-he-explore-other-careers/.

35 Ibid.

a cis white older man—which is westernized European culture, which is in and of itself its own expression," he said.

The problem is there are no official rules on what a lawmaker is supposed to wear inside the House chamber.

So, there's a very good chance someone might show up wearing a kilt, pantaloons, or heaven forbid—a loincloth.

GIANT BOULDER OFFENDS STUDENTS

The University of Wisconsin spent as much as $50,000 to remove a beloved seventy-ton boulder because students said it was racist.

I wish this was a *Babylon Bee* story, but it is not. The University of Wisconsin is run by morons.

It was a monument in honor of Thomas Chamberlin, a geologist who served as president of the university from 1887 to 1892. The Chamberlin Rock had been planted on Observatory Hill since 1925.

According to local news reports, the rock had previously been referenced by a derogatory nickname for any large dark rock some 85 years ago.[36]

University historians have not found any other time that the term was used, but they said the Ku Klux Klan was active on campus at that time, the Wisconsin State Journal reported.

The Black Student Union became emotionally triggered by the giant rock and led the charge to have it removed from the campus.

---

36 John Clark, "'Racist' Rock Removed from University of Wisconsin Madison Campus," MyStateline.com, August 6, 2021, https://www.mystateline.com/news/local-news/racist-rock-removed-from-university-of-wisconsin-madison-campus/.

"I'm grateful that we have had the opportunity to do this and that the rock will be removed," the group's president, Nalah McWhorter, said. "It was our demand, and it was something that we put all the work in for."

Using that flawed logic, every building on campus that was erected before the twenty-first century should be razed.

Student Juliana Bennett told ABC News that removing the rock signaled a small step toward a more inclusive campus.

"This moment is about the students, past and present, that relentlessly advocated for the removal of this racist monument," she actually said with a straight face. "Now is a moment for all of us BIPOC students to breathe a sigh of relief, to be proud of our endurance, and to begin healing."

University leaders praised the emotionally troubled students who were triggered by the giant rock.

"In the midst of demands for justice following George Floyd's murder last summer, the students wanted change on campus, and they worked hard to see this through," vice chancellor for student affairs Lori Reesor told reporters. "While the decision required compromise, I'm proud of the student leaders and the collaboration it took to get here."[37]

Those poor, wretched souls at the University of Wisconsin! Oh the horrors and mental anguish they must have suffered by walking by that boulder. It should've been smashed to smithereens and dumped in a river, but it was only moved to university-owned property.

---

37 Doug Erickson, "No Longer a Memorial, Rock Removed from Campus," University of Wisconsin–Madison News, August 6, 2021, https://news.wisc.edu/no-longer-a-memorial-rock-removed-from-campus/.

Sadly, alumni and students at the University of Wisconsin learned a very important lesson: never take your freedom for "granite."

HOME DEPOT CALLS OUT WHITE PRIVILEGE

Home Depot wants to fix white people and Christians.

The home improvement chain released a worksheet about white privilege. It was posted in the break room of a Canadian Home Depot.

If you're confident that the police exist to protect you—well, you have white privilege.

Home Depot also called out class privilege for you folks who went to college, cisgender privilege for you folks who know your pronouns, and if you get off for Christmas Day—Home Depot says you have Christian privilege.

"If you can use public bathrooms without stares, fear or anxiety, you have cisgender privilege," Home Depot said.

In other words, you're a very bad person if you have a problem with your little girl using the bathroom alongside a grown man wearing a dress and high heels.

The home improvement chain also called out able-bodied privilege and heterosexual privilege.

"If you don't have to explain that your spouse is of the same gender, you have heterosexual privilege," Home Depot Canada says. "If you don't have to worry about how to get into a store, you have able-bodied privilege."

Some of you might say, "What privilege?" You're working two jobs, living in a rental, driving a ten-year-old car, and eating off-brand peanut butter.

"White privilege does not mean your life has not been hard," the flyer states. "It simply means that the colour of your skin is not one of the reasons that makes it harder."[38]

Fortunately, all of you white, heterosexual, able-bodied, Christian fixer-uppers have the privilege of buying your power tools someplace else.

LAWMAKER SAYS JULY 4TH ONLY FOR WHITE PEOPLE

Rep. Cori Bush, the Democrat from Missouri, doesn't seem to think the United States of America is the most exceptional nation on Earth. Nor does she put much stock in us being the land of the free or the home of the brave.

On Independence Day, the black lawmaker posted a scathing rebuke of our great nation on Twitter.

"When they say that the 4th of July is about American freedom, remember this: the freedom they're referring to is for white people," the ungrateful Democrat wrote.[39]

"This land is stolen land and Black people still aren't free," she added.

For the record, the congresswoman intentionally capitalized "Black," while using lower case to refer to all of us "white" folks.

I reckon she put her white constituents in their lowercase place.

---

38 Ariel Zilber, "Home Depot Slammed for Shaming Employees for Their 'White Privilege,'" *New York Post*, March 23, 2022, https://nypost.com/2022/03/23/home-depot-ripped-for-shaming-employees-over-white-privilege/.

39 Samuel Chamberlain, "'Squad' Member Blasts July 4 Celebrations: 'Black People Still Aren't Free,'" *New York Post*, July 5, 2021, https://nypost.com/2021/07/05/rep-cori-bush-blasts-july-4-celebrations-black-people-still-arent-free/.

"If I as a white man slandered Juneteenth I would be called a racist," one disgusted citizen wrote on Facebook. "We have a sitting Congresswoman slandering the founding of this country in which she has benefited greatly and we are supposed to call her a Patriot? Sorry not happening."

Another wrote, "Maybe you should appreciate the country that gave you the platform to spew your hate, yes it needs work, yes it's not perfect, but it allows correction to 'make a more perfect union.'"

If, in fact, black people are not free, how was it possible for her to attend a private Catholic high school? How was it possible for her to graduate from a Lutheran nursing school? How was it possible for her to be elected to Congress if in fact she is still in chains?

Congresswoman Bush is free to spread her lies and spew her un-American venom because she happens to live in a free nation.

But if she is that oppressed, perhaps Ms. Bush would be more comfortable living in another nation. I'm sure she'd be welcomed with open arms in a third-world hellhole nation.

And to show there are no hard feelings, I'd even be willing to pay for her ticket. As a matter of fact, it would be my privilege.

The Democrats would have you believe that slaves are being bought and sold at Walmart and Costco.

But the truth is you cannot purchase a slave on American soil. There are no slave masters working the cotton fields of Mississippi. *Gone with the Wind* is long gone.

There's not a single person alive in our nation who has owned slaves or benefited from slavery. There's not a single black American today who has been enslaved by a white American.

We are a nation that has overcome one of the most heinous blemishes on our history. We fought a war to free the slaves. Blood was shed on American soil to ensure that all men were created equal.

We are a nation that once raised up a generation who had a dream—a dream of a society where men and women would be judged by the content of their character and not the color of their skin.

For a moment, that dream was realized.

But now our great nation is in the throes of yet another race war—this one specifically targeting white Americans. Schools are teaching children that they should apologize for their pigmentation.

Many companies are forcing white employees to denounce their so-called "white privilege." Anyone who opposes the full-scale destruction of historic monuments is labeled a racist or a white supremacist.

And now, the critical race theory mob is about to come after our bank accounts—reparations.

Representative Sheila Jackson Lee introduced a resolution to set up a committee to study and develop reparation proposals for African Americans. According to the bill's summary, the committee "shall examine slavery and discrimination in the colonies and the United States from 1619 to the present and recommend appropriate remedies."[40]

"The impact of slavery and its vestiges continues to affect African Americans and indeed all Americans in communities

40 "Commission to Study and Develop Reparation Proposals for African Americans Act," Bill, Congress.gov § (2021), https://www.congress.gov/bill/117th-congress/house-bill/40?s=1&r=6.

throughout our nation," Jackson Lee said in remarks reported by the *Washington Informer*.[41]

Former president Barack Hussein Obama has not fully endorsed the notion of taking money away from taxpayers and redistributing it to African Americans.

But he dabbled his big toe in that political pond over the spring and summer of 2022 during a podcast interview with alleged drunk driver Bruce Springsteen.

Obama blamed "the politics of white resistance and resentment" as the reason why he didn't push financial reparations for Black Americans during his presidency.

Obama said he believes reparations are "justified" and that "there's not much question that the wealth…the power of this country was built in significant part—not exclusively, maybe not even the majority of it, but a large portion of it—was built on the backs of slaves."

"We can't even get this country to provide decent schooling for inner-city kids," Obama said. "And what I saw during my presidency was the politics of white resistance and resentment. The talk of 'welfare queens' and the talk of the 'undeserving' poor. And the backlash against affirmative action. All that made the prospect of actually proposing any kind of coherent, meaningful reparations program…not only a non-starter but potentially counterproductive."[42]

---

41 Stacy M. Brown, "Rep. Sheila Jackson Lee Reintroduces Reparations Bill in New Congress," *Washington Informer*, January 4, 2021, https://www.washingtoninformer.com/rep-sheila-jackson-lee-reintroduces-reparations-bill-in-new-congress/.

42 Mark Moore, "Obama Says 'White Resentment' Made Reparations a 'Non-Starter' During Presidency," *New York Post*, February 25, 2021, https://nypost.com/2021/02/25/obama-reparations-were-non-starter-due-to-white-resentment/.

The White House has yet to say whether President Biden would throw his support behind a reparations bill, but don't be surprised if he does.

There are many people in this country who believe that working class Americans should share their paychecks with oppressed citizens like Oprah, Tyler Perry, LeBron James, and Maxine Waters.

I don't care if you are black or white, that's not reparations. That's thievery.

THE SOLUTION TO DEFEATING CRT

There's a simple solution to all of this critical race theory nonsense—fight back—fiercely!

Teachers in Arkansas will no longer be allowed to teach critical race theory.

Governor Sarah Huckabee Sanders signed an executive order that bans educators from teaching kids that black people are the oppressed and white people are the oppressors.

It's government-sanctioned indoctrination.

Gov. Sanders says schools need to get back to teaching reading, math, and science instead of white privilege and systemic racism.

And she promised voters that she would never allow taxpayer-funded schools to brainwash our kids with a far-left political agenda.

"Under my leadership, schools will teach reading, writing, math, and science—and our children will learn that the identity that truly matters is the one we all share: our identity as children of God and citizens of the United States of America," Huckabee said.

Needless to say the youngest governor in the nation has triggered the godless, heathen Left.

"What about immigrant children that aren't citizens yet? What if someone doesn't believe in God? Under your leadership you will force people to follow your beliefs through enacting unconstitutional laws," one angry critic wrote. "Tyrants like you are why people left Europe to come to America, a free nation."[43]

Another wrote, "Where is history, music, or art? God belongs in the church and at home. Our nation was founded upon separation of church and state. First amendment gives us freedom of and from religion. We are not a theocracy."

The Left fails to understand that the words "separation of church and state" are not a part of any founding document. Not a one. And that's because our Founding Fathers meant for the United States to be a nation who followed Judeo-Christian teachings.

And that—ladies and gentlemen—is how Republicans should govern. Stand on a firm foundation girded by the US Constitution and the Holy Bible.

43 Dan Whitfield (@DanWhitCongress), "What about immigrant children that aren't citizens yet?" Tweet, January 12, 2023, https://twitter.com/DanWhitCongress/status/1613746729928609793.

8

THIS IS GOD'S COUNTRY

IT'S IMPORTANT FOR Christian Americans to push back as happy warriors against the claims that America was founded as a secular nation. Just a cursory glance of our founding documents and the correspondence of our Founding Fathers should dispel any notion that we are anything but a country founded on Judeo-Christian philosophy.

Congressman Randy Forbes delivered a terrific recitation of the evidence in legislation he introduced more than a decade ago. It designated the first week of May as "America's Spiritual Heritage Week."

"When our Constitution was signed, the signers made sure that they punctuated the end of it by saying, 'in the year of our Lord, 1787,'" Forbes said in remarks on the House floor. "And 100 years later in the Supreme Court case of *Holy Trinity Church v. The United States*, the Supreme Court indicated, after recounting the long history of faith in this country, that we were even a Christian nation.

"President George Washington, John Adams, Thomas Jefferson, Andrew Jackson, Abraham Lincoln, William McKinley, Teddy Roosevelt, Woodrow Wilson, Herbert Hoover, Franklin

Roosevelt, Harry Truman, Dwight Eisenhower, John Kennedy, and Ronald Reagan all disagreed with the President's [Obama's] comments and indicated how the Bible and Judeo-Christian principles were so important in this nation," Forbes said. "And Franklin Roosevelt even led this nation in a six-minute prayer before the invasion of perhaps the greatest battle in history, the Invasion of Normandy, and asked for God's protection."[1]

He told CNS News at the time that the truths we hold to be self-evident come from our Creator.

"If we let people who want to challenge that convince us there is no Creator then we also have no rights," he said.

The congressman is correct. In 2020, Fox News Channel polled Americans about their impressions of our Founding Fathers. While a vast majority still see George Washington and Thomas Jefferson as revered figures in our history, a growing number said they are villains.

As I've written elsewhere in the book, our public schools are to blame. Our taxpayer-funded classrooms have been turned into indoctrination centers. Teachers are filling the minds of our children with lies and distortions about our great nation.

President Trump addressed that very issue during an Independence Day speech he delivered in 2020 in front of Mount Rushmore.

"Our nation is witnessing a merciless campaign to wipe out our history, defame our heroes, erase our values, and indoctrinate our children," he told the assembled crowd. "This attack on our liberty, our magnificent liberty, must be stopped."

---

1 U.S. House of Representatives, House Session, C-SPAN, May 6, 2009, https://www.c-span.org/video/?285755-1/house-session.

And education is the chief way to push back against the school house propaganda. On that note, I'd like to share with you the official bill presented by Congressman Forbes. It provides a terrific framework for educating next generation Americans about our Founding Fathers.[2]

> Affirming the rich spiritual and religious history of our Nation's founding and subsequent history and expressing support for designation of the first week in May as "America's Spiritual Heritage Week" for the appreciation of and education on America's history of religious faith.
>
> Whereas religious faith was not only important in official American life during the periods of discovery, exploration, colonization, and growth but has also been acknowledged and incorporated into all 3 branches of the Federal Government from their very beginning;
>
> Whereas the Supreme Court of the United States affirmed this self-evident fact in a unanimous ruling declaring "This is a religious people... From the discovery of this continent to the present hour, there is a single voice making this affirmation";
>
> Whereas political scientists have documented that the most frequently cited source in the

2 "H.Res.253 — 112th Congress (2011-2012)," https://www.congress.gov/bill/112th-congress/house-resolution/253/text?r=96&s=1.

political period known as The Founding Era was the Bible;

Whereas the first act of America's first Congress in 1774 was to ask a minister to open with prayer and to lead Congress in the reading of 4 chapters of the Bible;

Whereas Congress regularly attended church and Divine service together en masse;

Whereas throughout the American Founding, Congress frequently appropriated money for missionaries and for religious instruction, a practice that Congress repeated for decades after the passage of the Constitution and the First Amendment;

Whereas in 1776, Congress approved the Declaration of Independence with its 4 direct religious acknowledgments referring to God as the Creator ("All people are endowed by their Creator with certain unalienable rights, that among these are life, liberty and the pursuit of happiness"), the Lawgiver ("the laws of nature and nature's God"), the Judge ("appealing to the Supreme Judge of the world"), and the Protector ("with a firm reliance on the protection of Divine Providence");

Whereas upon approving the Declaration of Independence, John Adams declared that the

Fourth of July "ought to be commemorated as the day of deliverance by solemn acts of devotion to God Almighty";

Whereas 4 days after approving the Declaration, the Liberty Bell was rung;

Whereas the Liberty Bell was named for the Biblical inscription from Leviticus 25:10 emblazoned around it: "Proclaim liberty throughout the land, to all the inhabitants thereof";

Whereas in 1777, Congress, facing a National shortage of "Bibles for our schools, and families, and for the public worship of God in our churches," announced that they "desired to have a Bible printed under their care & by their encouragement" and therefore ordered 20,000 copies of the Bible to be imported "into the different ports of the States of the Union";

Whereas in 1782, Congress pursued a plan to print a Bible that would be "a neat edition of the Holy Scriptures for the use of schools" and therefore approved the production of the first English language Bible printed in America that contained the congressional endorsement that "the United States in Congress assembled... recommend this edition of the Bible to the inhabitants of the United States";

Whereas in 1782, Congress adopted (and has reaffirmed on numerous subsequent occasions) the National Seal with its Latin motto "Annuit Coeptis," meaning "God has favored our undertakings," along with the eye of Providence in a triangle over a pyramid, the eye and the motto "allude to the many signal interpositions of Providence in favor of the American cause";

Whereas the 1783 Treaty of Paris that officially ended the Revolution and established America as an independent begins with the appellation "In the name of the most holy and undivided Trinity";

Whereas in 1787, at the Constitutional Convention in Philadelphia, Benjamin Franklin declared, "God governs in the affairs of men. And if a sparrow cannot fall to the ground without His notice, is it probable that an empire can rise without His aid? ...Without His concurring aid, we shall succeed in this political building no better than the builders of Babel";

Whereas the delegates to the Constitutional Convention concluded their work by in effect placing a religious punctuation mark at the end of the Constitution in the Attestation Clause, noting not only that they had completed the work with "the unanimous consent of the States present" but they had done so "in the Year of our Lord one thousand seven hundred and eighty seven";

Whereas James Madison declared that he saw the finished Constitution as a product of "the finger of that Almighty Hand which has been so frequently and signally extended to our relief in the critical stages of the Revolution," and George Washington viewed it as "little short of a miracle," and Benjamin Franklin believed that its writing had been "influenced, guided, and governed by that omnipotent, omnipresent, and beneficent Ruler, in Whom all inferior spirits live, and move, and have their being";

Whereas, from 1787 to 1788, State conventions to ratify the United States Constitution not only began with prayer but even met in church buildings;

Whereas in 1795, during construction of the Capitol, a practice was instituted whereby "public worship is now regularly administered at the Capitol, every Sunday morning, at 11 o'clock";

Whereas in 1789, the first Federal Congress, the Congress that framed the Bill of Rights, including the First Amendment, appropriated Federal funds to pay chaplains to pray at the opening of all sessions, a practice that has continued to this day, with Congress not only funding its congressional chaplains but also the salaries and operations of more than 4,500 military chaplains;

Whereas in 1789, Congress, in the midst of framing the Bill of Rights and the First Amendment, passed the first Federal law touching education, declaring that "Religion, morality, and knowledge, being necessary to good government and the happiness of mankind, schools and the means of education shall forever be encouraged";

Whereas in 1789, on the same day that Congress finished drafting the First Amendment, it requested President Washington to declare a National day of prayer and thanksgiving, resulting in the first Federal official Thanksgiving proclamation that declared "it is the duty of all nations to acknowledge the providence of Almighty God, to obey His will, to be grateful for His benefits, and humbly to implore His protection and favor";

Whereas in 1800, Congress enacted naval regulations requiring that Divine service be performed twice every day aboard "all ships and vessels in the navy," with a sermon preached each Sunday;

Whereas in 1800, Congress approved the use of the just-completed Capitol structure as a church building, with Divine services to be held each

Sunday in the Hall of the House, alternately administered by the House and Senate chaplains;

Whereas in 1853, Congress declared that congressional chaplains have a "duty...to conduct religious services weekly in the Hall of the House of Representatives";

Whereas by 1867, the church at the Capitol was the largest church in Washington, DC, with up to 2,000 people a week attending Sunday service in the Hall of the House;

Whereas by 1815, over 2,000 official governmental calls to prayer had been issued at both the State and the Federal levels, with thousands more issued since 1815;

Whereas in 1853, the United States Senate declared that the Founding Fathers "had no fear or jealousy of religion itself, nor did they wish to see us an irreligious people...they did not intend to spread over all the public authorities and the whole public action of the nation the dead and revolting spectacle of atheistical apathy";

Whereas in 1854, the United States House of Representatives declared "It [religion] must be considered as the foundation on which the whole structure rests...Christianity; in its general principles, is the great conservative element on which we must rely for the purity and permanence of free institutions";

Whereas in 1864, by law Congress added "In God We Trust" to American coinage;

Whereas in 1864, Congress passed an act authorizing each State to display statues of 2 of its heroes in the United States Capitol, resulting in numerous statues of noted Christian clergymen and leaders at the Capitol, including Gospel ministers such as the Revs. James A. Garfield, John Peter Muhlenberg, Jonathan Trumbull, Roger Williams, Jason Lee, Marcus Whitman, and Martin Luther King Jr., Gospel theologians such as Roger Sherman, Catholic priests such as Father Damien, Jacques Marquette, Eusebio Kino, and Junipero Serra, Catholic nuns such as Mother Joseph, and numerous other religious leaders;

Whereas in 1870, the Federal Government made Christmas (a recognition of the birth of Christ, an event described by the U.S. Supreme Court as "acknowledged in the Western World for 20 centuries, and in this country by the people, the Executive Branch, Congress, and the courts for 2 centuries") and Thanksgiving as official holidays;

Whereas, beginning in 1904 and continuing for the next half-century, the Federal Gvernment [*sic*] printed and distributed The Life and Morals of Jesus of Nazareth for the use of Members of Congress because of the important teachings it contained;

Whereas in 1931, Congress by law adopted the Star-Spangled Banner as the official National Anthem, with its phrases such as "may the Heav'n-rescued land Praise the Power that hath made and preserved us a nation," and "this be our motto, 'In God is our trust!'";

Whereas in 1954, Congress by law added the phrase "one nation under God" to the Pledge of Allegiance;

Whereas in 1954, a special Congressional Prayer Room was added to the Capitol with a kneeling bench, an altar, an open Bible, an inspiring stained-glass window with George Washington kneeling in prayer, the declaration of Psalm 16:1: "Preserve me, O God, for in Thee do I put my trust," and the phrase "This Nation Under God" displayed above the kneeling, prayerful Washington;

Whereas in 1956, Congress by law made "In God We Trust" the National Motto, and added the phrase to American currency;

Whereas the constitutions of each of the 50 States, either in the preamble or body, explicitly recognize or express gratitude to God;

Whereas America's first Presidential Inauguration incorporated 7 specific religious activities, including—

(1) the use of the Bible to administer the oath;

(2) affirming the religious nature of the oath by the adding the prayer "So help me God!" to the oath;

(3) inaugural prayers offered by the President;

(4) religious content in the inaugural address;

(5) civil leaders calling the people to prayer or acknowledgment of God;

(6) inaugural worship services attended en masse by Congress as an official part of congressional activities; and

(7) clergy-led inaugural prayers, activities which have been replicated in whole or part by every subsequent President;

Whereas President George Washington declared "Of all the dispositions and habits which lead to political prosperity, religion and morality are indispensable supports";

Whereas President John Adams, one of only 2 signers of the Bill of Rights and First Amendment, declared "As the safety and prosperity of nations ultimately and essentially depend on the protection and the blessing of Almighty God, and the national acknowledgment of this truth is not only an indispensable duty which the people owe to Him";

Whereas President Jefferson not only attended Divine services at the Capitol throughout his presidency and had the Marine Band play at the services, but during his administration church services were also begun in the War Department and the Treasury Department, thus allowing worshippers on any given Sunday the choice to attend church at either the United States Capitol, the War Department, or the Treasury Department if they so desired;

Whereas Thomas Jefferson urged local governments to make land available specifically for Christian purposes, provided Federal funding for missionary work among Indian tribes, and declared that religious schools would receive "the patronage of the government";

Whereas President Andrew Jackson declared that the Bible "is the rock on which our Republic rests";

Whereas President Abraham Lincoln declared that the Bible "is the best gift God has given to men…But for it, we could not know right from wrong"

Whereas President William McKinley declared that "Our faith teaches us that there is no safer reliance than upon the God of our fathers, Who has so singularly favored the American people in every national trial and Who will not forsake us so long as we obey His commandments and walk humbly in His footsteps";

Whereas President Teddy Roosevelt declared "The Decalogue and the Golden Rule must stand as the foundation of every successful effort to better either our social or our political life";

Whereas President Woodrow Wilson declared that "America was born to exemplify that devotion to the elements of righteousness which are derived from the revelations of Holy Scripture";

Whereas President Herbert Hoover declared that "American life is builded, and can alone survive, upon…[the] fundamental philosophy announced by the Savior nineteen centuries ago";

Whereas President Franklin D. Roosevelt not only led the Nation in a 6 minute prayer during D-Day on June 6, 1944, but he also declared that "If we will not prepare to give all that we have and all that we are to preserve Christian civilization in our land, we shall go to destruction";

Whereas President Harry S. Truman declared that "The fundamental basis of this Nation's law was given to Moses on the Mount. The fundamental basis of our Bill of Rights comes from the teachings which we get from Exodus and St. Matthew, from Isaiah and St. Paul";

Whereas President Harry S. Truman told a group touring Washington, DC, that "You will see, as you make your rounds, that this Nation was established by men who believed in God. ...You will see the evidence of this deep religious faith on every hand";

Whereas President Dwight D. Eisenhower declared that "Without God there could be no American form of government, nor an American way of life. Recognition of the Supreme Being is the first, the most basic, expression of Americanism. Thus, the founding fathers of America saw it, and thus with God's help, it will continue to be" in a declaration later repeated with approval by President Gerald Ford;

Whereas President John F. Kennedy declared that "The rights of man come not from the generosity of the state but from the hand of God";

Whereas President Ronald Reagan, after noting "The Congress of the United States, in recognition of the unique contribution of the Bible in shaping the history and character of this Nation and so many of its citizens, has...requested the President to designate the year 1983 as the 'Year of the Bible'", officially declared 1983 as "The Year of the Bible";

Whereas every other President has similarly recognized the role of God and religious faith in the public life of America;

Whereas all sessions of the United States Supreme Court begin with the Court's Marshal announcing, "God save the United States and this honorable court";

Whereas a regular and integral part of official activities in the Federal courts, including the United States Supreme Court, was the inclusion of prayer by a minister of the Gospel;

Whereas the United States Supreme Court has declared throughout the course of our Nation's history that the United States is "a Christian country", "a Christian nation", "a Christian people", "a religious people whose institutions presuppose a Supreme Being", and that "we cannot read into the Bill of Rights a philosophy of hostility to religion";

Whereas Justice John Jay, an author of the Federalist Papers and original Justice of the United States Supreme Court, urged "The most effectual means of securing the continuance of our civil and religious liberties is always to remember with reverence and gratitude the Source from which they flow";

Whereas Justice James Wilson, a signer of the Constitution, declared that "Human law must rest its authority ultimately upon the authority of that law which is Divine...Far from being rivals or enemies, religion and law are twin sisters, friends, and mutual assistants";

Whereas Justice William Paterson, a signer of the Constitution, declared that "Religion and morality...[are] necessary to good government, good order, and good laws";

Whereas President George Washington, who passed into law the first legal acts organizing the Federal judiciary, asked, "where is the security for property, for reputation, for life, if the sense of religious obligation desert the oaths in the courts of justice?";

Whereas some of the most important monuments, buildings, and landmarks in Washington, DC, include religious words, symbols, and imagery;

Whereas in the United States Capitol the declaration "In God We Trust" is prominently displayed in both the United States House and Senate Chambers;

Whereas around the top of the walls in the House Chamber appear images of 23 great lawgivers from across the centuries, but Moses (the lawgiver, who—according to the Bible—originally received the law from God,) is the only lawgiver honored with a full face view, looking down on the proceedings of the House;

Whereas religious artwork is found throughout the United States Capitol, including in the Rotunda where the prayer service of Christopher Columbus, the Baptism of Pocahontas, and the prayer and Bible study of the Pilgrims are all prominently displayed; in the Cox Corridor of the Capitol where the words "America! God shed His grace on thee" are inscribed; at the east Senate entrance with the words "Annuit Coeptis" which is Latin for "God has favored our undertakings"; and in numerous other locations;

Whereas images of the Ten Commandments are found in many Federal buildings across Washington, DC, including in bronze in the floor of the National Archives; in a bronze statue of Moses in the Main Reading Room of the Library of Congress; in numerous locations at the U.S. Supreme Court, including in the frieze above the Justices, the oak door at the rear of the Chamber, the gable apex, and in dozens of locations on the bronze latticework surrounding the Supreme Court Bar seating;

Whereas in the Washington Monument not only are numerous Bible verses and religious acknowledgments carved on memorial blocks in the walls, including the phrases: "Holiness to the Lord" (Exodus 28:26, 30:30, Isaiah 23:18, Zechariah 14:20), "Search the Scriptures" (John 5:39), "The memory of the just is blessed" (Proverbs 10:7), "May Heaven to this Union continue its beneficence", and "In God We Trust", but the Latin inscription Laus Deo meaning "Praise be to God" is engraved on the monument's capstone;

Whereas of the 5 areas inside the Jefferson Memorial into which Jefferson's words have been carved, 4 are God-centered, including Jefferson's declaration that "God who gave us life gave us liberty. Can the liberties of a nation be secure when we have removed a conviction that these liberties are the gift of God? Indeed I tremble for my country when I reflect that God is just, that His justice cannot sleep forever";

Whereas the Lincoln Memorial contains numerous acknowledgments of God and citations of Bible verses, including the declarations that "we here highly resolve that…this nation under God…shall not perish from the earth"; "The Almighty has His own purposes. 'Woe unto the world because of offenses; for it must needs be that offenses come, but woe to that man by whom the offense cometh'" (Matthew 18:7), "as was said three thousand years ago, so still it must be said 'the judgments of the Lord are true and righteous altogether'" (Psalms 19:9), "one day every valley shall be exalted and every hill and mountain shall be made low, the rough places will be made plain, and the crooked places will be made straight and the glory of the Lord shall be revealed and all flesh see it together" (Dr. Martin Luther King's speech, based on Isaiah 40:4–5);

Whereas in the Library of Congress, The Giant Bible of Mainz, and The Gutenberg Bible are on prominent permanent display and etched on the walls are Bible verses, including: "The light shineth in darkness, and the darkness comprehendeth it not" (John 1:5), "Wisdom is the principal thing; therefore, get wisdom and with all thy getting, get understanding" (Proverbs 4:7), "What doth the Lord require of thee, but to do justly, and to love mercy, and to walk humbly with thy God" (Micah 6:8), and "The heavens declare the Glory of God, and the firmament showeth His handiwork" (Psalm 19:1);

Whereas numerous other of the most important American government leaders, institutions, monuments, buildings, and landmarks both openly acknowledge and incorporate religious words, symbols, and imagery into official venues;

Whereas such acknowledgments are even more frequent at the State and local level than at the Federal level, where thousands of such acknowledgments exist, and

Whereas the first week in May each year would be an appropriate week to designate as "America's Spiritual Heritage Week": Now, therefore, be it

Resolved, That the United States House of Representatives—

(1) affirms the rich spiritual and diverse religious history of our Nation's founding and subsequent history, including up to the current day;

(2) recognizes that the religious foundations of faith on which America was built are critical underpinnings of our Nation's most valuable institutions and form the inseparable foundation for America's representative processes, legal systems, and societal structures;

(3) rejects, in the strongest possible terms, any effort to remove, obscure, or purposely omit

such history from our Nation's public buildings and educational resources; and

(4) expresses support for designation of a "America's Spiritual Heritage Week" every year for the appreciation of and education on America's history of religious faith.

9

A LITTLE-KNOWN STORY ABOUT THE WASHINGTON MONUMENT

AS DAWN BREAKS over the Eastern Seaboard and the morning sun begins to spill its light across the waters of the Atlantic, there stands a monument of marble and granite rising high above our nation's capital.

The beacon rises more than 555 feet and provides a perfect panoramic view of the sixty-nine square miles that comprise the District of Columbia. To the north is the White House; to the south, the Jefferson Memorial; to the west, the Lincoln Memorial; and to the east, the Capitol. But no building is as tall as the obelisk.

At its pinnacle is a capstone made of aluminum. It was the intention of her architect, Robert Mills, to carve tributes on all four sides of the capstone—but it's the message he carved on the eastern side of the monument that holds the most importance.

The words have weathered time and turmoil, war and peace. To this day the seven letters Mr. Mills carved into the aluminum capstone remain:

Laus Deo

And when morning comes to America, the first rays of light illuminate the capstone—and Mr. Mills's testimony for the ages. You see the obelisk may celebrate a man, but it gives glory to a higher power—*Laus Deo*, praise be to God.

I think about the Washington Monument whenever I hear a godless heathen Democrat say that our nation is not a Christian nation. President Obama became the first commander-in-chief to make such an assertion during an interview with, ironically, the Christian Broadcasting Network.

It would not be the last time he made such a declaration.

> "I think that the United States and the West generally, we have to educate ourselves more effectively on Islam," he told a French television station in 2009. "And one of the points I want to make is, that if you actually took the number of Muslim Americans, we'd be one of the largest Muslim countries in the world."

Did you catch that? He said we'd be one of the largest Muslim countries in the world.

Obama reiterated his position in Turkey, where 98 percent of the nation is Muslim. The president, standing on foreign soil, declared the United States is not a Christian nation. "I've said before that one of the great strengths of the United States is, although as I mentioned we have a very large Christian population, we do not consider ourselves a Christian nation, or a Jewish nation or a Muslim nation," he said. "We consider ourselves a nation of citizens who are bound by ideals and a set of values."

The American public, though, disagrees with the president. A Gallup survey found that 78 percent of Americans consider themselves Christian. To be sure, the former president has his defenders. Among them is Michael Lind, the editor of *New American Contract*. In a column that appeared in Salon.com, he writes:

> "The American republic, as distinct from the American population, is not post-Christian because it was never Christian. In the president's words: 'We consider ourselves a nation of citizens who are bound by ideals and a set of values.' And for that we should thank the gods. All 20 of them."[1]

For what it's worth, John Adams, the second president of the United States, was pretty clear which of the "gods" to thank.

"July 4th, ought to be commemorated as the day of deliverance by solemn acts of devotion to God Almighty," he wrote in a letter to his wife, Abigail, on the day the Declaration of Independence was approved by Congress.

Obama's declaration stands in stark contrast to comments once made by former president Ronald Reagan.

"The Founding Fathers believed faith in God was the key to our being a good people and America's becoming a great nation," Reagan said.

And during a National Prayer Breakfast, Reagan did not hesitate to lay out the source of our nation's success.

"I also believe this blessed land was set apart in a very special way, a country created by men and women who came here not in search of gold, but in search of God," he said. "They would be free people, living under the law with faith in their Maker

---

1 Michael Lind, "America Is Not a Christian Nation," *Salon*, April 14, 2009, https://www.salon.com/2009/04/14/christian_nation/.

and their future. Sometimes, it seems we've strayed from that noble beginning, from our conviction that standards of right and wrong do exist and must be lived up to."

Not a Christian nation? Tell that to the men who wrote our Declaration of Independence. "We hold these truths to be self-evident, that all men are created equal, that they are endowed by their Creator with certain unalienable rights, that among these are life, liberty and the pursuit of happiness."

Not a Christian nation? Tell that to George Washington. He used fifty-four biblical terms to describe God in his various writings.

"While we are zealously performing the duties of good citizens and soldiers, we certainly ought not to be inattentive to the higher duties of religion. To the distinguished character of Patriot, it should be our highest glory to add the more distinguished character of Christian," he once wrote.

Not a Christian nation? Tell that to John Jay, the first chief justice of the Supreme Court. "Providence has given to our people the choice of their rulers, and it is the duty, as well as the privilege and interest of our Christian nation to select and prefer Christians for their rulers," he wrote.

Not a Christian nation? Tell that to James Madison, our fourth president and a signer of the US Constitution.

"A watchful eye must be kept on ourselves lest, while we are building ideal monuments of renown and bliss here, we neglect to have our names enrolled in the Annals of Heaven," he once wrote.

Not a Christian nation? Tell that to Daniel Webster who once argued before the Supreme Court in favor of teaching religious instruction to children.

"What is an oath? [I]t is founded on a degree of consciousness that there is a Power above us that will reward our virtues or punish our vices.... [O]ur system of oaths in all our courts, by which we hold liberty and property and all our rights, are founded on or rest on Christianity and a religious belief."

Not a Christian nation? Tell that to Patrick Henry, the voice of liberty.

"Being a Christian...is a character which I prize far above all this world has or can boast," he once said.

Not a Christian nation? Tell that to the father of the American Revolution, Samuel Adams.

"I conceive we cannot better express ourselves than by humbly supplicating the Supreme Ruler of the world...that the confusions that are and have been among the nations may be overruled by the promoting and speedily bringing in the holy and happy period when the kingdoms of our Lord and Savior Jesus Christ may be everywhere established, and the people willingly bow to the scepter of Him who is the Prince of Peace," he declared in a Fast Day Proclamation in 1797.

Not a Christian nation? Tell that to Benjamin Rush, a signer of the Declaration of Independence and the father of public schools under the Constitution.

"[T]he only means of establishing and perpetuating our republican forms of government is the universal education of our youth in the principles of Christianity by means of the Bible," he wrote.

Secular humanists may one day be successful in the religious cleansing of American history. We now live in a time when Christian values are being banished from the marketplace of ideas and expelled from our public schools. Many of our fellow believers have already paid a price for following the teachings of Jesus Christ.

But while the winds of change may sweep across the nation's capital—there stands a beacon of hope—a reminder that this nation of immigrants was built, not on sinking sand, but on a firm foundation, girded by Almighty God. And unless someone has a really tall ladder—and a blow torch—the first rays of morning light will shine down upon these United States of America illuminating an eternal truth and a grateful nation's prayer—praise be to God!

Laus Deo.

10

THE CHOCOLATE CZAR

BROWNIES ARE NOW banned in New York City schools. So are lemon bars, cotton candy—even carrot cake. The Big Apple is cracking down on childhood obesity by outlawing bake sales on school property. It's all part of the Education Department's efforts to force feed a wellness policy that also prohibits vendors from selling candy bars and potato chips in vending machines.

According to the mayor's office, about 50 percent of New York City youngsters are overweight. Somebody crunched the numbers and determined that chocolate pudding is making kids stupid—noting the correlation between student health and failing grades on standardized tests.

So now, vending machines are stocked with fruit juice and granola bars. And if the cheerleading team wants to earn money for new pom-poms, they'll have to sell carrot sticks and wheatgrass.

School leaders have given principals an incentive to force kids to eat healthy food. "Noncompliance may result in adverse impact on the principal's compliance performance rating," the policy states. In other words, that pudgy kid scarfing Oreos could cost a principal his job.

Howell Wechsler is the director of adolescent and school health at the Centers for Disease Control and Prevention. He told the *New York Times* the city's regulations are among the strictest in the nation. "Schools are supposed to be a place where we establish a model environment, and the last thing kids need is an extra source of pointless calories," he said.[1] For those of you reading between the lines, the good doctor is suggesting that the only place your child can definitely get a well-balanced meal is from the government.

I decided to check in with Smitty, my man down at City Hall and the mayor's point person on the candy crisis. Smitty is the director of New York City's Office of Chocolate Control Policy.

He promised to give me an inside look at the underbelly of a burgeoning crisis. So we set up a meeting at Mao Tse Tung Junior High School—ground zero in his quest to eradicate the sugary plague that has befallen our city.

"This is an epidemic," he said. "We believe it goes far beyond the walls of public schools. In many cases, children don't get their first taste of chocolate from their friends; they got it from their father or their mother's secret Valentine's Day stash."

"It sounds like a pretty serious problem," I said. "James Bond had Goldfinger, but you've got Butterfinger."

"You don't get it, Todd. America's war on teenage chocolate abuse will be won or lost in our schools. And that's why mandatory testing is a necessary. We can't rely on parents to do the right thing—so it's up to the government."

---

1 Jennifer Medina, "A Crackdown on Bake Sales in City Schools," *New York Times*, October 2, 2009, https://www.nytimes.com/2009/10/03/nyregion/03bakesale.html.

As was the case for drinkers during Prohibition, chocolate lovers have gone underground.

And that's certainly the case in the Big Apple. Smitty told me a black market has emerged. Chocolatiers have set up shop in dark alleys and in Central Park, offering kids milk chocolate morsels. The newspapers have been filled with heart-wrenching accounts of youngsters popping Skittles and snorting Pixie Sticks. The problem has become so severe, Smitty has recruited Lindsay Lohan, Britney Spears, and Paris Hilton to produce a series of public service announcements called, "Just say no to Ho Hos."

To illustrate his point, Smitty explained why he wanted to meet at Mao Tse Tung Junior High School. "We've isolated the heart of the contraband candy industry to this school," he said. "But so far, we've been unsuccessful in hunting down the leader."

"Sort of like a Godiva Godfather, I suppose."

"Very cunning," said Smitty. "The product is high grade. Very hard to track down. It melts in your mouth, not in your hands."

Many parents and students are quite upset. They defend the bake sales as a way to raise money for school uniforms and trips. I asked Smitty if extracurricular activities might suffer as a result of the ban.

"Oh, not at all," he replied. "We are providing the schools with some wonderful alternatives to bake sales. For example, children could sell environmentally friendly wrapping paper or adopt a tree."

Adopt a tree instead of nibbling on a snickerdoodle? Good luck with that.

Our conversation was interrupted by a series of bells and whistles blasting from the public address system.

"We have a Code Red in the boy's bathroom. I repeat, Code Red. Teachers, please lock your classroom doors. All security personnel to your stations!"

Smitty tossed me a Kevlar vest and ordered me to stay close as we sprinted down the hallway.

"What's happening? Has there been a shooting?"

"Worse," said Smitty. "We've got a kid with a candy bar. This might be the break we need."

The bathroom had already been secured by two guards who were busy mounting yellow crime scene tape around the entrance. Smitty flashed his Chocolate Czar credentials and immediately took charge.

"What do we have here, officer?"

"I caught the perpetrator red-handed," he said. "But he wouldn't cooperate, so I had to taser the boy."

Sure enough, there was a thirteen-year-old boy convulsing on the floor, his school books scattered under the urinals.

"Good grief, Smitty. He's just a boy. Was this really necessary?"

"This isn't some sort of school yard game, Todd. The War on Chocolate will have casualties. Now, somebody cuff the suspect."

Smitty rifled around inside the boy's backpack and pulled out what he thought was the smoking gun—a vial filled with colorful flakes.

"Fruity pebbles?" I asked.

Smitty, disappointed, tossed it aside. "No," he said. "Vitamins. Officer, I thought you said you caught him red-handed?"

"I did, sir. He tried to flush the evidence down the commode."

Smitty flung open the stall door and glanced into the toilet. About thirty seconds later, he ordered the officer to release the boy.

"I don't understand, sir. We have the goods on this perp. I caught him before he flushed the candy bar."

"Officer, I'm pretty certain that's not a Baby Ruth floating in there."

There you have it folks. Sometimes you feel like a nut, sometimes you don't.

11

THE BABY JESUS, PLANNED PARENTHOOD, AND THE WHITE HOUSE

IT REALLY SEEMED hard to believe. Did the White House really consider removing the Nativity from the East Room? If anyone knew the inside scoop, it was my buddy Smitty. He's a Washington institution. He was in the Beltway before there was a Beltway.

Smitty's occasional base of operation is a nondescript coffee house a few blocks from the White House. I caught the Delta Shuttle from New York City the other morning, took a cab from Reagan National Airport, and arrived at the coffee shop to find Smitty sequestered in a corner vinyl booth.

After exchanging pleasantries, I got right to the point—was the Nativity scuttlebutt really true?

Smitty's shoulders dropped, and he let out a long sigh.

"That was a very difficult situation," he admitted. "There were hours and hours of debate over what to do."

Well, that was a relief. At least it wasn't some sort of rash, last-minute decision.

"Hardly," he said. "The First Lady's social secretary actually commissioned a White House Special Committee on Whether the Nativity Was Politically Incorrect. Some of the nation's most well-respected atheists, agnostics, and Wiccans were invited to testify."

I thought it was a bit odd that the committee didn't have any religion experts, but Smitty's explanation seemed to make sense.

"There were some Constitutional issues," he said. "We wanted to respect the separation of church and state—but we certainly didn't want to alienate the other side. We reached a compromise by inviting esteemed religion professors from Harvard and Yale to testify."

Initially, he said the committee had considered keeping some of the main components of the Nativity. However, after much debate, that decision was considered problematic.

"Take Mary and Joseph for starters," he said. "We felt like leaving them would send the wrong message to sexually active teenagers."

"But didn't Mary give birth to her child? Doesn't the Christmas story contain a pro-life message?"

"Exactly," he said, pausing to take a sip of coffee. "And that was Planned Parenthood's point. So we decided it would be appropriate to remove Mary and Joseph."

"What about the three wise men?"

"Affirmative action issues," he replied. "There were also some concerns about diversity. Why were the only wise people men? Could there not have been a wise Latina? And don't even get me started on what happened with the shepherds."

I couldn't imagine what issues the White House would have had with shepherds tending their flocks.

"They weren't union," Smitty replied.

Based on my recollection of the Gospel of Luke, that left only a handful of characters—most notably the angels.

"Yeah, a chorus of flighty guys wearing dresses," Smitty said as he removed his glasses. "I don't need to tell you about the issues involving those stereotypes."

It seemed as though the only politically correct part of the Nativity was the livestock. "Well, that's what we thought too," he replied, as he wiped his glasses with a handkerchief. "The People for the Ethical Treatment of Animals signed off on the plan. They said it appeared the animals were well-cared for. But then, we received a cease and desist order from the Environmental Protection Agency."

The EPA?

Smitty motioned for me to move closer. He looked to his left, then his right before whispering in my ear. "It had something to do with the sheep," he said.

The sheep?

"According to a new government study, sheep pose a significant danger to the environment," he replied. "Our scientists have determined a twenty-pound sheep can release the equivalent of thirty-seven pounds of carbon dioxide."

Sheep gas? The federal government actually commissioned a study on sheep gas?

"It's nothing to joke about," he said. "A twenty-pound gassy sheep could blow a hole in the ozone."

By the end of the day, the White House Special Committee on Whether the Nativity Was Politically Incorrect eliminated Mary, Joseph, the Wise Men, the shepherds, the angelic choir, and the sheep. The only remaining component of the Nativity was the most important, and according to Smitty, it was the first to go—the Baby Jesus.

"That was a no-brainer," Smitty said. "Religion has absolutely no place in the Nativity."

And one would assume that was the end of the story, but we know that something miraculous happened in that meeting—something that saved the Christ child from eviction.

"You can thank Fannie Mae and Freddie Mac," he said. "Can you imagine the political ramifications of evicting an impoverished young family in this economy? The powers-that-be thought it would send an insensitive message to the electorate to do something like that—especially during the holiday season."

So, that's the inside scoop from the nation's capital, friends—at least the way it was told to me. The Nativity is safe for at least another yuletide season. But next December, don't be surprised if the folks at 1600 Pennsylvania Avenue are singing, "Away with the manger."

12

JERI-LYNN FROM GEORGIA SCHOOLS TODD ON "DEMON RATS"

SOME OF MY favorite callers are from the Southern states, and when I tangle on-air with a liberal, they are quick to respond. One of our fiercest defenders is "Jeri-Lynn from Georgia." More than once, she has been willing to snatch some leftist loon by the neck! One particular day, a gentleman named Harold accused me of being a Republican in Name Only (RINO). That did not sit well with Miss Jeri-Lynn or Grace Baker, my executive producer.

> Starnes: Jeri-Lynn, our good friend in Georgia WDUN, Jeri-Lynn, what say you?
>
> Jeri-Lynn: Well, hey, my sweet Todd and my love Grace. I just had to call in, Todd. I want to address your last caller, Mr. Harold, no disrespect whatsoever to him, but he is what's part of the problem with the RINOs. So if anyone's a RINO, Todd, it is Mr. Harold. Harold, I would like to say to you that you need to be following Todd Starnes. Because, Todd, this is why, besides

me loving you, and I am straightforward, you know that. I am not a Demon-rat, and I am not a Republican. I am now a straight blown conservative. And Todd, you and Steve Bannon are the only two that report facts and real news. So, Mr. Harold is in line with the RINOs, Mitt Romney, Mitch McConnell, and he needs to listen to you more, and then he would realize that you're the only one that gives us truth. So, Harold, you need to go do whatever, plant your garden, honey, whatever you want to do and join the rest of the RINOs cause all of us that listen to Todd Starnes out here know for a fact that he is nothing but truth. And you are so far off that he's a RINO. Why doesn't he go join Biden, the biggest idiot demon-rat ever nominated, Harold? That's what I got to say, Todd Starnes.

Starnes: Jeri Lynn, well look.

Jeri-Lynn: He done made me angry, honey, calling you a RINO. Oh, my goodness.

Starnes: Jeri Lynn, now you put me in a position where I think I have to defend Harold. I don't think Harold is a RINO. I just think he doesn't understand the point of me sharing that polling data. It's not that I believe the data, but it's a reminder that we've got to be focused. We can't take anything for granted. And look, I don't know who they're talking to. I've never gotten a call from one of these pollsters, but it does serve a purpose, and that's the purpose.

Jeri-Lynn: Todd, me and millions of others tune in to hear you and what you have to say every single day. So no, I'm sorry, you can defend Harold all you want. But, honey, Harold, go plow your garden. Honey, go play in your garden, honey, and stay out of politics. You should not be voting, if that's what you think.

Starnes: Jeri-Lynn, are you doing well otherwise, Miss Jeri?

Jeri-Lynn: I love you, Todd Starnes.

Starnes: It's okay, Jerri-Lynn, are you doing okay otherwise?

Jeri-Lynn: Talking about my Todd and Grace, honey, I'm telling you, I'll slap the brisket off your tongue. I'm trying to be a Christian, Todd. He ruffled my feathers.

Starnes: Jeri-Lynn, God bless you, you see this? This is the best part of our show is we have the kindest, most ferocious callers out there. And Jerri-Lynn, you're one of our favorites. God bless you. When we come through to Gainesville, you got to drop by and say hello.

Jeri-Lynn: You better believe I will, Todd. I love you and Miss Grace. And like I say, Todd, you're the last person standing that tells us the truth. You don't tell us what we want to hear, you tell us what we need to hear.

Starnes: We do our best.

Jeri-Lynn: I love you, Todd, and I appreciate you greatly. Don't let Harold ruin your day.

Starnes: You take care of yourself, alright, Miss Jeri-Lynn. We're going to put her in charge of security, Grace.

Grace Baker: I think that's a great idea.

13
STARNES GETS SENT TO THE HENHOUSE

A FEDERAL JURY has convicted renowned journalist Todd Starnes of the mass genocide of chickens. Starnes was the first American tried under a new federal law that gives animals the right to sue human beings.

Starnes, who once declared that the only good chicken is a fried chicken, faces twenty-five years in prison. His punishment could have been worse. However, since he only ate white meat, prosecutors were not able to charge him under federal hate crime statutes.

The jury, made up of a dozen barnyard animals, also found him guilty on aggravated assault charges. According to investigators, several of his victims were battered before being deep-fried.

People for the Ethical Treatment of Animals (PETA) hailed the ruling.

"We proudly stand alongside our poultry brothers and sisters," said a PETA spokesperson. "America's chickens can roost in peace tonight. Their clucks have been heard."

According to a Gallup poll, almost a third of Americans believe animals should be given the same rights as people. Some 62 percent say animals deserved some protections but could still be used for the benefit of humans—either grilled or deep-fried one must assume.

The renowned American philosopher Martha Nussbaum told the *Daily Express* that animals must have equal rights with humans.

"Animals are not things that we may use as we like," she said. "They are sentient beings who seek their own lives. We share this fragile globe with many other animals, who also feel pain, suffer loss, desire companionship, and to put it briefly, who want to live their own lives just as we want to live our lives."

The star witness for the government was Cass Sunstein, who once served as the nation's first livestock czar. He was widely credited with giving animals the right to sue humans—a move that led to the arrest of Starnes.

"Human's willingness to subject animals to unjustified suffering will be seen as a form of unconscionable barbarity," he said, quoting a speech he delivered in 2007 at Harvard University. "It's morally akin to slavery and the mass extermination of human beings."

However, Starnes had several high-profile witnesses in his corner—among them, the Chick-fil-A cow, who placed his hoof on the Bible and swore to tell the truth.

"Eat more chicken," the bovine declared, bringing an immediate objection from the prosecution and swift condemnation from Judge Rabinowitz.

"Hate speech against poultry will not be tolerated in this courtroom—not even from a bovine," said the visibly angry judge.

One of the more emotional moments came when Earl the Chicken's widow took the witness stand. She described their life together on the farm and how he taught his chicks that the early bird always gets the worm.

However, defense attorneys raised several questions about her husband's character.

"Isn't it true, ma'am, that your husband was known to associate with other hens in the hen house?"

"Cluck," she clucked.

"And isn't it true that he was known for being something of a hothead—scratching around the barnyard—ruffling feathers?"

"Cluck, cluck," she clucked.

"And furthermore, isn't it true that on the day of his alleged demise, your husband, Earl the Chicken, was a suspect in the mysterious death of a Kentucky colonel known for wearing white suits and black string ties?"

At that point, Mrs. Chicken began squawking uncontrollably. "Ba-gock!"

The judge slammed down his gavel.

"That's it," he shouted. "I will have order in this court. The chicken is excused—and will the prosecution please instruct your client to refrain from laying eggs in the witness stand?"

After a brief recess to collect the eggs, Judge Rabinowitz brought back the jury and asked the court reporter to read back some of the bird's testimony.

"I'll do my best, your honor, but it's going to be difficult," she said. "Why's that, Sally? Forget your reading glasses?"

"No, your honor—it's the writing. It's chicken scratch."

The turning point in the trial came when a forensic scientist from the New York City CSI found what would become the damning evidence against Starnes.

"We searched the defendant's apartment and found what appeared to be the final resting place for Mister Chicken," said Special Agent Casey Culver. "The evidence was scattered across a kitchen counter—chicken pieces were everywhere. Most had been discarded in a cardboard bucket with red and white stripes."

"Were there any condiments?"

"Not to my knowledge, sir—but we did find a side of slaw."

The prosecutor probed Agent Culver for more information about the crime scene.

"It was one of the most horrendous crime scenes I've ever had to navigate, sir," he said. "We found, we found—I'm sorry—it was just so traumatic."

The prosecutor walked back to his table, grabbed a bottle of water, and handed it to the emotionally distraught agent.

"Take your time, son," he said. "Now, tell us. What did you find?" "We found appendages sir."

"Appendages?"

"Yes sir. Chicken appendages—and what appeared to be dipping sauces."

The courtroom erupted into a chorus of gasps and several outbursts, leading the judge to gavel the crowd into submission.

"Order," he said. "I will have order in my courtroom." And that's when the special agent dropped the bombshell.

"We found evidence some of the victims were exposed to some sort of chemicals before they were deep fried," said Special Agent Casey Culver.

"What kind of chemicals?" the prosecutor asked.

"We aren't quite certain," Culver replied. "But we've been able to isolate at least eleven herbs and spices."

In spite of the overwhelming physical and circumstantial evidence, Judge Rabinowitz nearly had to declare a mistrial after an unfortunate incident involving the jury. The house cat ate the parakeet, forcing the judge to install an alternate juror.

It took the jury five minutes to render a verdict.

"Mister Starnes, you've been found guilty of a most fowl crime—the genocide of Earl the Chicken and his offspring. Sir, your behavior is a disgrace to mankind. Do you have any last words before I sentence you?"

Starnes stood alongside his attorney and was immediately surrounded by US Marshals.

He looked down at the table and then turned to face Judge Rabinowitz.

"Yes, your honor," he replied in a hushed courtroom. "I do have something to say." "Well, we're waiting," the judge said.

Starnes adjusted his glasses, straightened his tie, and cleared his throat.

"Those chickens were finger-licking good," he replied.

14

TRANS-SPECIES SWIMMER MAKES HISTORY

PHILADELPHIA 2050 (AP)—A trans-species swimmer swept the 2050 Ivy League Swimming and Diving Championships.

Flipper, a dolphin that identifies as a woman, also broke every record in the history of women's swimming.

The trans-species swimmer was also named ESPN's Female Athlete of the Year and was chosen to appear on the front of *Sports Illustrated*'s annual swimsuit edition.

The dolphin's athletic success brought back memories of Lia Thomas, the male swimmer who pioneered the transgender athletic movement.

Mr. Thomas, who was a lackluster male swimmer ranked 462, broke a number of longstanding records in women's swimming back in the early years of the twentieth century.

He actually tied biological female Riley Gaines in the NCAA Division I Women's Championships. Instead of giving both athletes a trophy, the NCAA awarded Mr. Thomas the hardware.

Ms. Gaines, who swam for the University of Kentucky, was flabbergasted.

She told Fox News that female swimmers were forced to endure all sorts of hostility from Mr. Thomas both in the pool and the locker room.

"We were not forewarned beforehand that we would be sharing a locker room with Lia. We did not give our consent, they did not ask for our consent, but in that locker room we turned around, and there's a six foot four biological man dropping his pants and watching us undress, and we were exposed to male genitalia," Gaines said.

Likewise, there was an unfortunate issue of Flipper exposing his blowhole during at least one nationally televised swim meet. Regardless, Flipper eventually became a spokesfish for the Democrat Party's most sacred plank—denying biology.

In 2028, President Chelsea Clinton signed into law her mother's signature legislation, the Equality Act. The legislation cleared the way for the sex and gender revolutionaries to obliterate gender norms in women's sports.

By the year 2030, most coaches had replaced all biological women with transgender athletes.

"What else were we supposed to do," said legendary WNBA Coach Jolene "Butch" McConkle. "It's hard to win games when the other team is putting five gals on the court, six-foot-ten with Duck Dynasty beards. They weren't exactly classically beautiful, but boy could they dunk those balls."

The league fell on hard times during the biological women era of the WNBA, but all that changed when men who identified as women signed up to play.

"The ovaries were an obstacle," Coach McConkle said.

Soon, there was a mass exodus of players from the NBA all but willing to transition into the WNBA.

At its zenith, the once-floundering basketball league exploded with newfound girl power featuring superstars like LaBrea James and Stephanie Curry, not to mention old school players like Charlene Barkley and Karen Abdul-Jabbar.

"I've never felt so liberated with my ball-handling," Queen LaBrea told *Sports Illustrated.*

But the athletic career of Flipper has been anything but smooth sailing. Critics pounced on reports that the mammal is just not that good of a swimmer.

"Out of five hundred dolphins in his pod, Flipper came in dead last," said one source who asked to remain anonymous. "But when she's swimming with the humans, she comes in first place."

The nation's LGBT+ (Ladyfish, Guppy, Bass, Tuna) community is outraged over the lack of support from the human population. They say Flipper has been traumatized by hate mail and is the victim of delfiniphobia, which, according to Tyra Banks, is a real thing.

"Flipper has had a difficult life," one close ally said. "She grew up in a single-family ocean after her father was mistaken for a tuna on an episode of the reality television show *Wicked Tuna*."

"You can't imagine how traumatic it is to watch a loved one get shoved into a tuna can on national television," the ally added. "But these latest attacks are just offensive. They say Flipper has artificial fins and that she's been in an inappropriate relationship with Aquaman."

And that's why the best human swimmer in the NCAA is in fact a dolphin.

Holy mackerel, America.

15

THE REAL QUESTION WE SHOULD BE ASKING ABOUT DRAG QUEENS

A FEW MONTHS ago, a Twitter mob accused me of being homophobic because I described a big burly man wearing a dress as a big burly man wearing a dress. One of the far-left media watchdog groups threatened to write a story.

"Why did you call that person a 'big burly man in a dress,'" the aggrieved writer demanded to know.

I replied, "Because it was a big burly man in a dress—and had I wanted to be rude, I would've mentioned that his pantyhose were riding up his butt crack and that an off-the-shoulder paisley top is just not a good look for a big-boned man."

They never published the story.

Now, I have a slightly different take on the matter of drag queens, and it's caused a bit of grief among my fellow evangelicals. I believe that under the United States Constitution, a person is free to live their life how they see fit—provided they are not infringing upon my civil liberties.

So, if Darlene Clodhopper, formerly known as Doug, wants to open up a drag bar and play the soundtrack from *Mamma Mia* twenty-four hours a day, I say grab a feather boa and have at it. Well, everything but the *Mamma Mia* part. I have an aversion to Swedish rock bands.

And it seems to me that the folks who should be hollering the loudest about the drag queens taking over our public libraries and grade schools are the law-abiding, tax-paying drag bar owners of America. Technically, they are now in competition with the federal and state governments.

The issue is not the eighteen-and-over crowd—it's the eighteen-and-under crowd. Why is the government and why are the alphabet activists so determined to get preschoolers to embrace drag queens?

And why is law enforcement turning the other way when the drag queens invite children to insert dollar bills into their spandex-encased crotches?

Left to their own devices, I contend that children embrace their boyhood or girlhood at a very young age. It comes to them naturally. And that's why the alphabet activists are so anxious to begin their grooming in preschools and kindergartens.

Michigan Attorney General Dana Nessel told the *Detroit News* that that she wanted a "drag queen in every school."

Nessel, who is gay, said, "Drag queens make everything better. Drag queens are fun."

New York City, meanwhile, is spending more than $200,000 to bring drag queens into the schools for "drag queen story hours." School leaders promised that the shows would be "fabulous." That's a word they use a lot in the drag industry.

But it turns out many New York City parents did not see the fabulousness in the city's decision to keep parents out of the loop.

"I didn't get any notice," parent Reese Harrington told the *New York Post*. "My daughter actually came home and told me that a drag queen came to the school…I feel like it would have been better for that conversation to happen at home."[1]

"I can't believe this. I am shocked," public school mom Helen Qiu said. "I would be furious if he was exposed without my consent. This is not part of the curriculum."

City Council member Vicki Paladino, a Republican from Queens (the home of Archie Bunker) said she was considering pulling funding to any public school that sponsors a drag queen story hour.

"We are taking hundreds of thousands of dollars out of the pockets of hardworking New York taxpayers…to fund a program teaching little children about their gender fluidity? Not on my watch," she told the *Post*.

RuPaul, the infamous television drag queen star, all but signaled his intentions during a speech he delivered on the Emmy awards broadcast.

"Thanks to all of our lovely children on our show from around the world," RuPaul said. "They are so gracious to tell their stories of courage and how to navigate this difficult life even more difficult today."[2]

"This is for you and you kids out there watching," he said.

"You have a tribe that is waiting for you," he said. "We are waiting for you, baby. Come on to Mama Ru."

---

1 Mary Kay Linge and Jon Levine, "Over $200k Being Spent on Drag Queen Shows at NYC Schools, Records Show," *New York Post*, June 11, 2022, https://nypost.com/2022/06/11/over-200k-being-spent-on-drag-queen-shows-at-nyc-schools/.

2 Proma Khosla, "RuPaul Is Now the Most Decorated Black Artist in Emmys History," Mashable, October 19, 2021, https://mashable.com/article/rupaul-emmys-win-history.

Are you paying attention, moms and dads?

In 2018, a Louisiana drag queen defended drag queen story time to city leaders during a meeting in Lafayette.

"This is going to be the grooming of the next generation. We are trying to groom the next generation," the drag queen declared as shocked parents gasped.[3]

Drag queen story time is not *Mister Rogers' Neighborhood*, folks. Nor is it *Sesame Street* with sequins. It's a government-sanctioned freak show paid for with your tax dollars.

If parents want to take their toddlers to a drag queen show they should head down to the local gay bar, not the taxpayer-funded public library.

Your children are being exposed to a highly funded propaganda campaign at the highest levels of power in Hollywood and Washington, DC. And the following stories I've compiled over the past several years will affirm my assertion.

UNIVERSITY WELCOMES DRAG QUEENS, NOT GOD

The University of Central Oklahoma (UCO) has opened its arms to drag queen shows and safe sex carnivals, but they draw the line at Christians who believe God created the Heavens and the Earth in six days.

The university has no problem with students tossing dildos through cardboard vaginas, but they draw the line at exposing impressionable young minds to the teachings of a creationist.

Ken Ham, the founder of the popular Creation Museum and Ark Encounter, was disinvited from speaking on the public

3 "Drag Queens out to 'Groom' Your Kids," Chick Publications, 2019, https://www.chick.com/battle-cry/article?id=drag-queens-out-to-groom-your-kids.

university campus after an ugly campaign of bullying by LGBT activists.

I obtained exclusive emails between the UCO Student Association and Answers in Genesis explaining why they had to rescind the invitation and opt out of a signed and legally binding contract.

"We are currently getting bombarded with complaints from our LGBT community about Ken Ham speaking on our campus," student body president Stockton Duvall wrote. "I was going to request that Mr. Ham refrains from talking on this issue, even if asked his views during the Q&A."

Ham was supposed to deliver his remarks in, of all places, the university's Constitution Hall.

"I find it highly ironic that after being booked to speak in the school's Constitution Hall, our constitutional right to free speech and the exercise of religion, guaranteed under the First Amendment, have been denied," Ham said.

"While I know this looks awful censoring certain parts of Mr. Ham's views, I want to ensure that we stay on topic of the research Mr. Ham and his team have done over creationism," Duvall wrote.

For the record, Ham's lecture was titled, "Genesis and the State of the Culture."

Paul Blair, the pastor of a local church that sponsors a student ministry called "Valid Worldview," told me Ham's speech had nothing to do with LGBT issues.

"The backlash we are already receiving is quite immense and I do not want this event to be spoiled due to a topic that isn't relative to Mr. Ham's research of creationism," Duvall wrote.

"A small but vocal group on campus put up a fuss about my talk and the university caved in, tearing up the contract and contradicting its policies of promoting 'free inquiry' and 'inclusiveness' on campus," Ham said.

Pastor Blair told me he does not fault the student government association president for caving in to the LGBT mob.

"I think this young man was bullied and intimidated," Blair said. "I think he succumbed to the bullying that these LGBTQ groups are known for. Those that scream out and demand tolerance are in actuality the least tolerant group of individuals on the planet."

A university spokesman told me there had been no complaints of LGBT bullying.

"The UCO community is an inclusive environment that encourages the civil expression of diverse thoughts and ideas, while also keeping the safety of our students a top priority," the spokesman said.

Blair, the pastor of Fairview Baptist Church, pointed out the university's blatant hypocrisy and what he called "the obvious discrimination against Christianity on campus."

"I am beside myself with frustration that our tax dollars go to promote a drag queen show and safe sex events with carnival games that are obscene and graphic," he said. "Yet when it comes to something like debating Darwinian evolution or talking about the literal Creation account of Genesis—well that kind of speech must be censored."

The pastor has a valid point.

If the University of Central Oklahoma expects Christian students to be tolerant of LGBT-themed events, why aren't they demanding that same expectation from LGBT students when it comes to Christian events?

SCHOOL TAKES KIDS TO DRAG SHOW

Parents in Chester County, Pennsylvania, signed permission slips allowing their kids to attend a local theater's production of *Alice in Wonderland.*

But instead of the Cheshire Cat, the kids got a look-see at an award-winning drag queen. And parents are madder than a hatter. They say the school never mentioned that a man dressed up like a woman would be a part of the show.

Permission slips mention that the goal of the trip was to develop an understanding of plot and dialogue. And the school district suggested in a statement that parents had a responsibility to read the biographies of the performers.

"In advance of the performance, families were informed that students had the opportunity to attend a contemporary, pantomime version of Alice in Wonderland and given permission slips to return. The actors' biographies and acting credentials were not included with this information but were accessible on the People's Light and Theater website," the school district wrote in a message to Broad and Liberty.[4]

It's a fair point that parents should always do their homework because public schools are no longer interested in transparency. They're on the side of the sex perverts, not mommy or daddy.

---

4 Beth Ann Rosica, "Beth Ann Rosica: Alice in Drag - Curiouser and Curiouser When It Becomes a School Field Trip," Broad + Liberty, December 6, 2022, https://broadandliberty.com/2022/12/06/beth-ann-rosica-alice-in-drag-curiouser-and-curiouser-when-it-becomes-a-school-field-trip/.

The great irony is that Lewis Carroll, the author of *Alice in Wonderland*, was a conservative. He was also a deacon in the Church of England. So it's unlikely he intended for a drag queen to make a guest appearance in *Wonderland*.

The least the school district could've done is alert parents that the production was not a traditional performance of *Alice in Wonderland* and that their youngsters would be exposed to twerking by a dude dressed as a feline.

FAMILY-FRIENDLY DRAG SHOW WAS ANYTHING BUT FRIENDLY

Parents in Chattanooga, Tennessee, were horrified after video surfaced of a so-called "family-friendly" drag show at the Wanderlinger Brewing Company.[5] The video shows a small child stroking what appeared to be the private parts of a person dressed like a Disney princess.

The "child-friendly" event included a "princess meet & greet," along with a drag queen story time.

Supporters of the drag queens blasted critics—accusing them of being intolerant homophobes.

"Right-wing nutjobs should just stay in their churches," said one defender. "This is nothing more than a talent competition and no different than a beauty pageant."

Most of the city seemed to disagree with that assessment.

"This is a crime," said one observer.

---

5 "'Drag Queen' Viral Video at Wanderlinger Brewing Company Sparks Controversy," Local 3 News, September 27, 2022, https://www.local3news.com/local-news/drag-queen-viral-video-at-wanderlinger-brewing-company-sparks-controversy/article_e5c0df24-3dec-11ed-81d0-af25941e754e.html.

A number of people wondered why a brewing company would host a drag show for children when they won't even allow people under the age of twenty-one to access its website.[6]

"You need to be of legal drinking age to visit our website," reads a warning on the brewing company's page.

The provocative performance was part of Chattanooga Pride Youth Day.

"So we now just stand by and let establishments host drag shows for all ages," one astonished resident wrote on social media. "We let children watch kink/stripper style dancing and call it gender affirmation? We have breweries/bars host events for Youth watching these events who will no doubt encouraged by parents to hand dollar bills to adults removing clothing items and shaking their bums in thongs?"

Hundreds of Chattanoogans took to social media to express their disgust and horror that any adult (male or female) would allow a child to touch his private parts.

"I'd like to see how the crowd reacts if a normal dude is onstage and has a little girl rub his crotch. But throw a dress on him and it's ok," wrote one outraged woman on Facebook. "The fact that a grown adult, no matter what they're wearing, would allow a child to stroke their private area is beyond disgusting."

And some longtime customers said they will never return to the brewery.

"This is so infuriating," one customer wrote. "I have been a mug club member and loved this brewery. I have messaged them that I will never come back. I encourage my local friends to never

---

6 "WanderLinger Brewing Company," WanderLinger Brewing Company, accessed September 24, 2023, https://www.wanderlinger.com/.

walk in Wanderlinger and support a place that exposes kids to this disgusting practice."

Another wrote, "Drag queens dancing in front of children or anyone for that matter is disgusting and should be banned. I hope you change your wicked ways or lose a lot of business."

MEMPHIS SCIENCE MUSEUM TURNS INTO DRAG VENUE

The Museum of Science and History (MoSH) announced they would host their first-ever family-friendly drag show. Promotional materials about the event read:

> Presenting the Museum of Science & History's grand culmination of our Summer of Pride programming and a celebration of the LGBTQ+ community, the FIRST EVER MoSH DRAG SHOW! This historic show will star a diverse cast of performers featuring different styles, expressions, and identities, showcasing some of the infinite ways in which we can manifest the art of drag. After the show, we'll kick off our intergenerational dance party, where everyone is invited to come together and dance the night away. Join us for a night of art, music, dance, and community at the museum.
>
> The program will feature performances from Fendi LaFemme, Angel Fartz, Barbie Wyre, Shaklina, Trixie Thunder and Siren Moss.

Word of the drag show sparked a massive backlash against the museum. Staffers were compared to "child-abusing degenerates," "perverts in dresses," groomers, and morons.

"Disgusting. How you could try to say this is family friendly is deceitful. Stick to science and history. You'll be losing so much more revenue than you ever thought because of this," one angry supporter of the museum wrote on social media.

"This is not family friendly," wrote another. "Why is this being done at the museum? There is zero educational content in this. This belongs in an adult club. I'm appalled."

And another pointed out that a drag show is "not family friendly."

"What does this have to do with science or history," the person wondered.

A museum staffer replied to one of the inquiries noting that they were trying to provide a welcoming environment. The staffer also pointed out that there are no places in Memphis where children under the age of eighteen can attend a drag show.

That message has since been deleted.

"Our children are being indoctrinated all around us. What parent would take his/her child to a drag show," wrote one upset patron. "God help us! We are Sodom and Gomorrah for sure."

Parents, church leaders, and school teachers should be warned that in recent months the museum has undergone a radical transformation by sex and gender revolutionaries.

MoSH previously hosted an exhibit titled, "Rise Up: Stonewall & The LGBTQ Rights Movement."

Museum leaders have also produced a podcast titled, *A Queer Understanding*. Interviews were conducted with Aubrey Ombre, a drag queen and trans advocate. Miss Mothie, another drag queen, described his journey to "self-discovery."

The museum also featured an exhibit titled, "Memphis Proud: The Resilience of a Southern LGBTQ+ Community."

Even more puzzling for moms and dads was the museum's summer film series. It had nothing to do with science.

"The Summer Pride Film Series" included rated-R movies with LGBT themes like *Swan Song*, *The Decadence With Love*, and *Moonlight*, a film about a young man growing up in Miami grappling with his identity and sexuality.

What any of this has to do with encouraging boys and girls to become interested in science is beyond me.

They say that MoSH stands for the Museum of Science and History. But they should consider rebranding the taxpayer-funded facility as the Museum of Sex and Hijinks.

DRAG QUEENS MOUNT GIANT EGGPLANT

Los Angeles held its gay pride parade in 2022, and it was just as horrifying as you might imagine. They engaged in behavior I'm not allowed under federal law to even describe on the radio.

In the crowd were hundreds of small children, and they were exposed to pornographic debauchery that would've made Hugh Hefner blush.

One parade float featured a drag queen mounted atop a giant eggplant—surrounded by scantily clad men.

"We have genitals and lube," the drag queen announced to the crowd.

We are living in a society where right is wrong, wrong is right, and not even the produce section of your grocery store can escape the sex and gender revolutionaries.

It's okay for children to read storybooks promoting gender confusion, but *The Cat in the Hat* is racially offensive.

It's okay for grown men to parade around nearly naked in the streets, but it's against the law for a football coach to pray in public.

It's okay for drag queens to groom children inside classrooms where the name of God has been banished.

Our nation is heading down a very dangerous path, as described in the New Testament book of Romans:

> Because of this, God gave them over to shameful lusts. Even their women exchanged natural sexual relations for unnatural ones. In the same way the men also abandoned natural relations with women and were inflamed with lust for one another. Men committed shameful acts with other men, and received in themselves the due penalty for their error. Furthermore, just as they did not think it worthwhile to retain the knowledge of God, so God gave them over to a depraved mind, so that they do what ought not to be done. They have become filled with every kind of wickedness, evil, greed and depravity. They are full of envy, murder, strife, deceit and malice. They are gossips, slanderers, God-haters, insolent, arrogant and boastful; they invent ways of doing evil; they disobey their parents; they have

> no understanding, no fidelity, no love, no mercy. Although they know God's righteous decree that those who do such things deserve death, they not only continue to do these very things but also approve of those who practice them.
>
> Romans 1:26–32 (NIV)

KIDS DRAGGED TO PRIDE EVENT IN DALLAS

Parents around the nation are disgusted, outraged, and a bit nauseous after watching a video of scantily-clad drag queens shaking their groove thang in front of children.

Mr. Misster, a gay nightclub in Dallas, hosted "Drag the Kids to Pride," an event that was clearly meant to introduce children to the drag culture—men dressing as scantily clad women and dancing for cash.

The drag queens performed in front of a giant pink neon sign reading, "IT'S NOT GONNA LICK ITSELF!"

Even more disturbing, a video shows the drag queens, some of whom were dressed in thongs, taking dollar bills from children and parents.

One woman protesting says she saw a poster for the event and was emboldened to come out and protest.

"I live in this community," the woman told television station WFAA.[7] "I have for several years. I don't believe that I should be seeing signs advertising for children to be dancing on stage with

7 Jay Wallis, "Dallas Protesters Show up to 'Drag the Kids to Pride' Family-Friendly Drag Show," WFAA, June 4, 2022, https://www.wfaa.com/article/news/local/dallas-family-friendly-kids-drag-show-mr-misster-protest/287-c7984c66-6141-4690-97b1-ec0b9882b4bb.

men in thongs and in inappropriate clothing and makeup. I do not in any way condone the behavior that these people are engaging in, but what drags me out here is it's kids now."

Protesters gathered outside the gay bar holding signs reading, "Stop grooming the kids."

But the organizers of the event said it had nothing to do with grooming children. Instead, they say it was a "family-friendly" drag show.

"We host our Champagne Drag Brunch every Saturday at 2pm for guests that are 21+ but we have partnered with some of our major community partners to host a special Pride Drag Brunch for all guests, including guests that couldn't normally attend our regular show because of the drinking age restriction, to raise money for a local LGBTQ+ youth organization," they wrote in a statement.[8]

I contend that if you are a grown adult, you have a constitutional right to live your life however you want to live your life. If you want to be a drag queen, grab a feather boa and have at it. If you want to be an exotic dancer at a strip club, well, that's your constitutional right as well.

But to expose children to gay bars and, yes, strip clubs, is nothing short of child endangerment.

And parents who expose their children to this sort of debauchery should be arrested and charged with child abuse.

Central Park School for Children in North Carolina also held a week-long celebration of gay pride where they are urging boys and girls to "liberate themselves." My friend, the journalist

8 Brody Levesque, "'Stop Grooming the Kids,' Right-Wing Protests Dallas Drag Event at Gay Bar," Los Angeles Blade, June 5, 2022, https://www.losangelesblade.com/2022/06/05/stop-grooming-the-kids-right-wingers-protest-dallas-drag-event-at-gay-bar/.

A. P. Dillon, exposed this insanity during an interview on my radio program.

The charter school hosted a Pride and Liberation Event for boys and girls in grades K through eight. The children learned all about the LGBTQ movement—from drag queens to something called queer history.

The drag queen—known as Justin Clapp—is an advocate of something called anti-transphobia. And he says anyone who feels uncomfortable around a drag queen is a bigot.

"We put forward a social justice bent, with a focus on humor, enthusiastic consent, antiracism, antitransphobia, antimisogyny, just basically trying to create an environment for everyone. And I think anyone who has been to our shows has felt comfortable, unless they are a bigot," Clapp told *Indy Week* in 2018.[9]

"The e-mail also said that they didn't want teachers to tell this to the parents until they had actually rolled it out. So parents were going to be getting blindsided, so I decided that I would go ahead and publish this," Dillon said.

The Raleigh *News & Observer* reports the pride and liberation event was in response to bullying at the school, in a story titled "Gay kids were getting bullied. So an NC school called in the drag queens."[10]

According to the email, the purpose of the pride and liberation event is:

---

9 Allison Hussey, "Drag Queen Vivica C. Coxx Has a Big Personality. the Change She Effects Is Even Bigger.," INDY Week, September 27, 2019, https://indyweek.com/guides/archives-guides/drag-queen-vivica-c-coxx-big-personality-change-effects-even-bigger/.

10 Shelbi Polk, "Gay Kids Were Getting Bullied. So an NC School Called in the Drag Queens.," The News & Observer, May 30, 2019, https://www.newsobserver.com/news/local/article230394199.html.

1. Increased visibility for queer members of the community, with a focus on centering queer People of Color.

2. Education on race, gender, queer history, and intersectionality, as well as advocacy, contributing to spaces of inclusiveness and liberation, and upstanding/anti-bullying.

3. Challenging common misconceptions and the increasing instances of exclusionary, demeaning, and threatening language and actions amongst students, disproportionately affecting students of Color, LGBTQ students, and female students.

This is what radical indoctrination looks like, folks. Why else would you expose five-year-old children to drag queens, and why else would you try to "liberate" a kindergartner?

Grade school children should be learning how to read and write and multiply. But instead, they are being subjected to ideas and concepts they are far too young to understand.

DRAG QUEEN THREATENS VIOLENCE

A Memphis drag queen threatened violence if Tennessee Governor Bill Lee signed a bill that would ban children from attending drag performances. The governor did in fact sign the bill.

The new law classifies "male and female impersonators" as adult cabaret performers and bans "adult-oriented performances that are harmful to minors," as defined in Tennessee's obscenity law. Those who violate the law would face fines up to $3,000 and possible prison time.

Drag queen Slade Kyle says the law is intended to strip away his rights.

He urged people at a Memphis night club to fight back, invoking the Stonewall Riots of the 1960s.

"The original Pride was a riot, and this year we need to remind them that we will fight for our liberation," Kyle said in a video. "We will raise our bricks up high again and let them know that we will not go quietly."

During the 1969 Stonewall Riots, protesters threw bricks at officers—injuring four.

Kyle told Buzzfeed that transgender activists like Marsha P. Johnson and Sylvia Rivera are inspiring drag performers across the state to fight back. Johnson and Rivera were credited with throwing the first brick at police during the Stonewall riots, Fox News reported.[11]

"It's a reminder that we will fight for our freedom, if necessary. It's not a threat. It's a promise," Kyle said. "And I am terrified to have to hold that promise…but we have to fight even if we're terrified. Nobody wants to have to be the next Marsha P. Johnson."

Understand what Kyle is saying. If four-year-olds cannot attend drag shows, they will take up arms against the government. That's how committed the radical activists are to grooming and indoctrinating your children.

---

11 Yael Halon, "Tenn. Drag Queen, Citing 1969 Stonewall Riot, Vows to Fight Back If Ban Passes: 'Not a Threat but a Promise,'" Fox News, February 27, 2023, https://www.foxnews.com/media/drag-queen-citing-1969-stonewall-riot-vows-fight-back-ban-passes-not-threat-promise.

As I mentioned in a previous chapter, the San Francisco Gay Men's Chorus once performed a song titled "We're Coming For Your Children."

I would take them at their word.

TEXAS TOWN PICKS DRAG QUEENS OVER BABY JESUS IN CHRISTMAS PARADE

For the past decade, the ministerial alliance in Taylor, Texas, has partnered with City Hall to produce an annual Christmas parade.

But that partnership was severed after pastors objected to a float filled with drag queens singing Christmas carols.

The ministers said parade entrants must be consistent with traditional biblical and family values. They determined drag queens did not fit those values.

"We do not feel like drag queens dancing in the Christmas parade, that these are the values we want to communicate to our children," Pastor Jeff Ripple told the *Washington Post*.[12]

The Taylor Area Ministerial Alliance (TAMA) posted a lengthy message on the ministerial association's Facebook page:

> TAMA has hosted Taylor's only Christmas Parade for years. All people and all families, no matter what they look like, are welcome to enjoy the parade. The Taylor Christmas Parade of Lights is a celebration of the birth of Jesus. TAMA is an organization of churches that holds to traditional Biblical and family values. We want to make sure all entries do not contradict those values. Last year

12 Molly Hennessy-Fiske and Eva Ruth Moravec, "A Texas Culture Clash: Dueling Parades over the Meaning of Christmas," *Washington Post*, December 4, 2022, https://www.washingtonpost.com/nation/2022/12/04/texas-holiday-parade-drag/.

Taylor Pride, a recently formed group made it into the parade due to an unfortunate oversight on our part. To be clear, the group known as Taylor Pride, which seeks to promote the LBGTQ+ lifestyle as biblically accepted, with two men inappropriately dressed as women, should never have been allowed to participate and put their promotion on display to families who had no warning about what was coming. That being said, it has always been the case for our Christmas parade that business, organizations, religious or government schools, political organizations, groups, individuals, etc. who have participated in the past have absolutely no requirement to be Christian or religious. Further, there have been no Christian or religious theme requirements for floats and that remains completely unchanged. We have had many participants who would disagree with our Biblical and traditional beliefs and that is perfectly fine. That is no problem for us. That has not changed at all this year. All are welcome to participate, however, as an explicitly Biblical organization, this year TAMA has taken steps to ensure that no participant under the Taylor Area Ministerial Alliance explicitly contradicts, with their entry, what our entire organization is built on, the Word of God. Further, our views of what is "family-friendly" are in step with what would have been the plainly accepted and agreed upon definition up until very recently. On the other hand, up until very recently, the idea of gaudy and overtly sexualized transvestites being put on public display during a parade which celebrates the Biblical event of Jesus Christ being born into this world to save sinners like all of us, would understandably have been unthinkable. TAMA's parade will continue like normal. We will do something to make it clear when our family-friendly parade is over and the City's parade begins. The traditional Taylor Christmas Parade of Lights will go on.[13]

"I don't hate LGBTQ individuals. I don't hate adulterers. There's lots of sin out there. I believe the most loving thing I can do is tell people the truth," the pastor said. "That if they don't repent of their sin—and that's any sinner—they will spend an eternity separated from God."

That decision sparked a huge culture war fight in the small Texas town.

The *Washington Post* reports that the school district barred students from marching in the parade. The Chamber of Commerce pulled out, as did City Hall.[14]

"We couldn't co-sponsor an event that wasn't open to everybody in the city," city spokesperson Stacey Osborne told the *Washington Post.* "Not only did we not want to open up the city to any type of legal action, but more importantly we have worked hard to make the city a welcoming place."

City leaders then announced they would host a separate parade that was open to everyone—including drag queens.

---

13 Taylor Area Ministerial Alliance, "TAMA has hosted Taylor's only Christmas Parade for years," Facebook post, November 14, 2022, https://www.facebook.com/taylorareaministerialalliance/posts/2368032903355463/?paipv=0&eav=AfZORsagNNUi7G1V9PlmmqYqvC-jFG2DXddij9uLAuoxDS5xuHSCrddk0owQHx_1I_A&_rdr.

14 Hennessy-Fiske and Moravec, "A Texas Culture Clash: Dueling Parades over the Meaning of Christmas."

But that was still not good enough for the local LGBT activists.

Denise Rodgers, president of Taylor Pride, told the *Post* that while the group has received local support, she wished the city had pulled the ministers' parade permit.

"Just the fact that they are allowed to have this exclusive parade on public property is already breaking the rules," Rodgers said of the ministers' group. "They have to choose a side. Because this has become a hate group. And we saw what happened with that…in Colorado."

The pastors refused to back down, and they refused to forsake the Gospel message for the gospel of inclusivity.

No doubt that jingled somebody's bells.

MARYLAND SCHOOLS TO TEACH KIDS ABOUT DRAG QUEENS

Maryland's largest school district unveiled a LGBTQ book list for elementary students that teaches four-year-olds about drag queens and fifth graders about transgenderism.

Montgomery County Public Schools (MCPS) presented the reading material in a PowerPoint presentation to teachers as a part of a professional development workshop on the topic of "Building Community with LGBTQ+ Affirming Picture Books."

The school district promoted the workshop, saying the new book list is designed to "reduce stigmatization and marginalization of transgender and gender nonconforming students," per a Fox News report.[15]

---

15 Jessica Chasmar, "Maryland School District Unveils LGBTQ Book List That Teaches Words 'Intersex,' 'Drag Queen' to Pre-K Students," Fox News, November 15, 2022, https://www.foxnews.com/politics/maryland-school-district-unveils-lgbtq-book-list-teaches-words-intersex-drag-queen-pre-k-students.

"All students deserve to see themselves in their school and classroom, including students who identify as LGBTQ+ and come from LGBTQ+ headed families and have family members that are a part of the LGBTQ+ community," the presentation states.

"There are no planned explicit lessons related to gender and sexuality, but these books do mean that LGBTQ+ identities will be made visible. Inclusive curricula support a student's ability to empathize, connect, and collaborate with a diverse group of peers, and encourage respect for all," the PowerPoint says.

The presentation adds that no one who "does not agree or understand" a student's gender identity will be urged to change their opinion.

"No child, or adult, who does not agree with or understand another student's gender identity or expression or their sexuality identity is asked to change how they feel about it."

MCPS recommended specific books for each grade level, each year increasing the sexual content. For instance, kindergarten teachers in the district are being told to read their students *Pride Puppy*, a book that teaches children about drag queens and being intersex.

When the students are around the age of five or six, teachers are supposed to read *Uncle Bobby's Wedding* with the children. In this story, "Uncle Bobby" gets married to another man. MCPS says this story will teach children to "recognize that people's multiple identities interact and create unique and complex individuals," according to the MCPS guide.[16]

---

16 Fox News, "Maryland School District Unveils LGBTQ Book List That Teaches Words 'Intersex,' 'Drag Queen' to Pre-K Students," *New York* Post, November 15, 2022, https://nypost.com/2022/11/15/maryland-school-district-unveils-lgbtq-library-for-pre-k-5th-grade/.

By the time the students reach fifth grade, they are supposed to read *Born Ready*, a story about a transgender child.

The MCPS guide says the district hopes that when students read this book, they will notice "how happy Penelope is when his mom hears him and commits to sharing with their loved ones that he is a boy—say again that we know ourselves best."

The workshop instructs teachers to tell parents they can't opt their children out of the readings and class discussions, saying the lessons are not about sex or anatomy but instead about diversity.

Additionally, teachers are told they should scold students who ask legitimate questions about the radical lessons. The presentation provides a sample comment from a student who says, "That's weird, he can't be a boy if he was born a girl. What body parts do they have?"

The school district's suggested answer to such a question reads, "That comment is hurtful; we shouldn't use negative words to talk about peoples' identities. Sometimes when we learn information that is different from what we always thought, it can be confusing and hard to process. When we are born, people make a guess about our gender and label us 'boy' or 'girl' based on our body parts. Sometimes they're right, and sometimes they're wrong."

The example response continues to tell students that physical anatomy does not decide gender.

"Our body parts do not decide our gender. Our gender comes from inside—we might feel different than what people tell us we are. We know ourselves best," the response concludes.

MCPS told Fox the materials are age-appropriate, and parents will be notified of their usage in the classroom.

"As part of MCPS' mission to equity, 'instructional materials are chosen to reflect the diversity of our global community, the aspirations, issues and achievements of women, persons with disabilities, persons from diverse, racial, ethnic, and cultural backgrounds, as well as persons of diverse gender identity, gender expression, or sexual orientation,'" the school district added.

FEDS SPENDING TAXPAYER CASH ON FOREIGN DRAG QUEENS

There is great outrage among American taxpayers over the news that American tax dollars have been used to fund drag queen performances in Ecuador.

The US Department of State has awarded more than $20,000 for a cultural center in Ecuador to host "drag theater performances" in the name of diversity and inclusion, Fox News first reported.[17]

"This is just sick," Rep. Ronny Jackson (R-TX) wrote in a Tweet. "This is how your tax dollars get spent under Biden. These degenerates must be defeated in November."[18]

"I'm speechless," said Rep. Pat Fallon (R-TX). "Taxpayer dollars are funding drag shows in Ecuador."

Why is Biden's State Department putting our tax dollars into the thongs of Ecuadorian drag queens? Although I'm surprised there's not more of an outcry from American drag queens—I have to imagine that many of them are suffering financially because of

---

17 Jessica Chasmar, "State Dept Defends $20K Grant for Drag Shows in Ecuador," Fox News, October 23, 2022, https://www.foxnews.com/politics/state-dept-defends-20k-grant-drag-shows-ecuador.

18 Ronny Jackson (@RonnyJacksonTX), "It's just been discovered that our very own State Department is sending tens of thousands of dollars to fund drag shows overseas," Tweet, October 19, 2022, https://twitter.com/RonnyJacksonTX/status/1582863662624432128.

inflation. There's just not enough dollars in their thongs to pay for the gallons of makeup and glitter they need to get gussied up."

FISHER-PRICE SELLING DRAG QUEEN DOLLS FOR KIDS

Fisher-Price wants your child to become a drag queen.

The national toy maker has introduced a collection of dolls that promote cross dressing and the drag queen lifestyle: the *RuPaul's Drag Race* edition of the Little People Collection—figurines in pink and purple gowns with flamboyant hairdos.

Monica Cole, director of One Million Moms, is stunned, accusing Fisher-Price of pushing an LGBT agenda on small kids: grooming the next generation—following a trend in public education to introduce two- and three-year-olds to radical sex and gender philosophies.

"It is outrageous that a toy company is marketing and normalizing gender dysphoria to young children. Parents who are not already aware of the company's agenda, please be forewarned: Children are being 'groomed' by Fisher-Price drag queen dolls under the disguise of playtime," Cole said.[19]

"Fisher-Price is purposely confusing our innocent children by attempting to destroy very definitive gender lines," she said.

Cole continued, "Liberal manufacturer Fisher-Price is following a culturally popular trend to desensitize America by telling children they can be whatever gender they want to be. This irresponsible line of toys is dangerous to the well-being of our children. Fisher-Price should avoid an obvious attempt to please a small percentage of customers while pushing away conservative

19 Monica Cole, "Mattel Pushes Transgender Barbie," American Family Association, June 24, 2022, https://afa.net/the-stand/culture/2022/06/mattel-pushes-transgender-barbie/.

customers who hold to the age-old truth that a boy is a boy, and a girl is a girl."

Mattel—the parent company of Fisher-Price—defended the drag queen toy line.

"RuPaul is a pop-culture icon who has been hailed as the best-dressed queen on TV and is coming to life in a whole new way for lip-syncing, runway-slaying fans," a statement from the company read.[20]

They say the collectibles are meant to send a message to not be afraid of making yourself over in your own image.

"Why can't the toy manufacturer let kids be who God created them to be instead of glamorizing a sinful lifestyle?" Cole asked.

Someone should tell Fisher-Price that God creates male and female—without feather boas.

NINE-YEAR-OLD DRAG QUEEN PROMPTS LAWMAKERS TO TAKE ACTION

Lawmakers in Ohio considered a piece of legislation that would ban children from performing in drag at Buckeye State bars.

Republican Tim Schaffer introduced the bill after stories surfaced about a nine-year-old boy who performed a sexually explicit dance routine at a bar while patrons gave the child money.

Here's how the *Toledo Blade* described the incident: "Critics of a video shared online objected to the boy's costume, which included a leotard and wig, dance moves characterized as sexual

---

20 Alexander Kacala, "Sashay into the Playroom! Fisher-Price Unveils Fabulous RuPaul Toy Set," TODAY, May 11, 2022, https://www.today.com/popculture/popculture/sashay-playroom-fisher-price-unveils-fabulous-rupaul-toy-set-rcna28317.

in nature, and that the boy can be seen accepting money from bar patrons during the performance."[21]

Schaffer said the performance was akin to sexual exploitation. The bill also has support from some Democrats.

The proposed legislation would expand the definition of child endangering to include "a performance that suggests a minor is participating in, or simulating, sexual activity that 'taken as a whole by the average person applying contemporary standards, appeals to the prurient interest.'"

But the child's mother is furious—she says there's nothing wrong with her son dressing in drag. And there's nothing sexual about his performance.

Jake "is just a guy who likes to dress up and dance and feel pretty," she told the *Toledo Blade*. "It's kind of like Halloween every time he has the opportunity to do it.

"He's in an unusual situation in that he's surrounded by people who are supportive. Ninety-five percent of our friends are in the LGBTQ community and are drag queens, and are in some type of theater performance," the mother told the newspaper.

LGBT activists in Toledo agree with the mom—and say the boy's performance was blown out of proportion. They said there is nothing inappropriate about a nine-year-old dressing in drag and dancing in a club.

"I think on its face [the bill] sounds good, but the intent and where the proposal came from was done in bad faith," Harvey House board president Kristen Angelo told the newspaper.

---

21 Lauren Lindstrom and Jim Provance, "Ohio Legislation Proposed after Perrysburg Boy's Drag Show," Toledo Blade, April 19, 2019, https://www.toledoblade.com/local/politics/2019/04/19/ohio-tim-schaffer-proposes-house-bill-180-banning-sexually-suggestive-performance/stories/20190419137.

"There is nothing wrong with what [he] is doing. Nothing sexual, nothing inappropriate."

Just let that sink in for a minute, moms and dads. There's nothing inappropriate about a nine-year-old performing at a bar? Apparently, Ohio needs legislation to dictate what should be basic common sense—and decency.

My friend Tony Perkins is president of the Family Research Council. He's been a consistent and bold voice for traditional values in this great nation. He was a guest on my radio program a while back discussing his outrage over a drag show for children in of all places Dallas, Texas. He explained that the issue really does go back to something we discussed earlier in the book. It's about parenting.

"That's a part of the problem, Todd. It goes back to the fact that parents are not engaged completely in the lives of their children. They're not guarding them. And what they're being exposed to and they're being led to believe that this stuff is harmless when in fact it's not. In fact, I'll go ahead and say it. You'll probably be criticized, but this is grooming," he said. "We are allowing these predators to groom children in many ways and also to prepare them for sexual confusion."

And that brings me back to the question I posited at the beginning of this chapter. The question that no one in the drive-by media is asking. It's not whether drag shows should be held in public libraries or grade schools. The question is, why are grown men who twirl around in sequins so obsessed with performing in front of children?

16

THE GREAT BARBECUE BAILOUT OF 2023

WASHINGTON THE PRESIDENT ASSERTED unprecedented government control over the nation's barbecue industry today by authorizing a billion-dollar bailout of pit masters hit hard by an outbreak of swine flu and rising labor costs.

"It's appropriate for the federal government to assume control over the nation's barbecue joints," said Earl Butts, the president's recently appointed pork czar. "Who knows more about pork than Congress?"

"Right now, our nation's barbecue restaurants are not moving in the right direction fast enough to succeed," said Butts, who warned that the country was on the verge of a pork apocalypse.

"The president has said it before, and I will repeat," he said. "We can't allow pulled pork to simply vanish. We've got to make sure it is there and the pit masters and hog farmers and cardiologists who rely on the industry stay in business."

The decision marked a turning point for an industry hit hard by the swine flu outbreak as well as allegations of racism. In 2022, the pork industry was forced to abandon its long-held slogan, "The other white meat," after a national boycott by some civil rights groups.

Earlier this year, the Centers for Disease Control launched a massive campaign to reassure Americans in the wake of the flu outbreak by increasing production of a special swine flu vaccine.

"Americans who took two spoonfuls of barbecue sauce and a side of slaw were able to stave off the symptoms," Butts said.

The secretary of Health and Human Services held a national press conference to inform the country it was still okay to pull pork. She went so far as to demonstrate how to wipe the sauce from one's mouth—not with your hands but on your shirt sleeve.

However, the damage was already done—leading to the government takeover. It's only the latest in a string of industries to be federalized. Since the early days of the administration, the government has engineered takeovers of Fannie Mae, Freddie Mac, the insurance giant American International Group, and General Motors.

"We cannot afford to see this industry collapse," Butts said. "There is a real concern that could happen."

But some restaurant owners objected to the plan, suggesting pork unions were to blame for the industry's woes.

"Union wages are killing us," said Clyde Marcel, owner of the Memphis-based restaurant, Rib Ticklers. "We're forced to pay our employees on average $75 an hour. We can't pull enough pork to pay the bills."

To cover the cost of wages and pension benefits, many barbecue restaurants have had to pass along enormous price increases to their customers. The average cost of a rack of ribs nationwide is $150, not including wet wipes.

"These pension plans are killing us," Marcel said. "What right do our employees have to live high on the hog? And don't even get me started on the health care benefits. Do you know how much I'm shelling out for cholesterol coverage?"

As a result, many American consumers have turned to cheaper alternatives, specifically South Korean barbecue.

"It's just not right," said Marcel. "It's bad enough we've got to deal with folks in California who want to barbecue tofu. If the Good Lord wanted barbecue to be made in South Korea, he wouldn't have created Memphis."

There is growing opposition on Capitol Hill, as well.

"It crosses a line," said one southern congressman who asked not to be identified. "It's not about saving a way of life. This is about saving the politically powerful pork unions."

Others wonder where the line should be drawn. Should the government save Memphis barbecue or Kansas City barbecue? Wet or dry rub? Carolina mustard or Virginia vinegar?

"This is just a waste of taxpayer money," another lawmaker said. "Pork barrel spending at its worst, and the president's pork czar is to blame."

Butts was the owner of the Butt Rubbers Barbecue Palace prior to his appointment as the White House pork czar. His restaurant's motto was, "We rub pork—mostly."

In 2005, he was the focus of a sexual harassment investigation filed by two former waitresses. The alleged Butts made them wear T-shirts that read, "Nice rack."

Those charges were dismissed when investigators determined the slogan referred to the ribs and not the waitresses.

He was also the subject of massive protests by animal rights groups after he said the only good animal "is a grilled animal."

Regardless, Butts earned the president's affection by perfecting a recipe for barbecuing arugula and was appointed despite congressional opposition.

He deflected criticism of the government bailout and called critics of the program "anti-meat."

"The barbecue industry historically has been the backbone of America's restaurant base," Butts said. "And we're going to do everything in our power to make sure it stays that way.

"The president believes Congress did the right thing, and his attitude is that any additional money we put into the barbecue industry, any help we provide, is designed to ensure a long-term sustainable industry and not just kicking the sauce down the road."

Meanwhile, the White House poultry czar is considering plans for an unprecedented bailout of the nation's chicken restaurants. Administration officials have named the project, "Cash for Cluckers."

17

DISNEY IS THE WOKEST PLACE ON EARTH

WALT DISNEY HAS been cancelled by Walt Disney.

When Disneyland first opened in 1955, Walt Disney delivered a speech welcoming people to the happiest place on Earth:

> To all who come to this happy place: Welcome. Disneyland is your land. Here age relives fond memories of the past, and here youth may savor the challenge and promise of the future. Disneyland is dedicated to the ideals, the dreams and the hard facts that have created America with the hope that it will be a source of joy and inspiration to all the world. Thank you.
>
> —Walt Disney

For sixty-seven years, that speech was delivered—but not this year.

Disney won't say why they made the change, but I'm going to go out on a limb and suggest that the word that triggered the woke Disney execs was "America."

The *New York Post* found that many Disney fans agreed with my perspective.

Walt's speech invokes "the ideals, the dreams and the hard facts that have created America," which one Twitter user called "taboo" for Disney's "woke" agenda.

"Because it mentions both history and facts, two things that are taboo to the woke agenda," the user tweeted, adding an excerpt of the speech.

"Terrible. Today the company seems to only use Walt as a marketing opportunity and not as a guiding force. What reason they had to cut this speech? I have no idea. @Disneyland do better," wrote another user.[1]

Disney has been on something of a cultural purge of late—banning pronouns and gender-specific language. Guests are no longer welcomed as "ladies and gentlemen" or "boys and girls."

They also took religious Christmas carols out of their annual holiday celebration.

And it's all by design, according to Latoya Raveneau, a writer-producer-director at Disney. She boasted about her "not-at-all-secret gay agenda" in a leaked video obtained by journalist Christopher Rufo.

"I was just, where I could, adding queerness," she said. "If you see anything queer in the show, no one would stop me, and no one was trying to stop me."

Sadly, Disneyland is really not the happiest place on Earth anymore—and I blame the cancel culture mob.

---

1 Alexandra Steigrad, "Fans Blame 'Wokeness' as Disneyland Cuts Walt Speech from Anniversary," *New York Post*, July 19, 2022, https://nypost.com/2022/07/19/disneyland-anniversary-cuts-walt-speech-fans-cry-wokeness/.

"Walt is rolling over in his grave. Wokeness has infected and damaged Disney," one user wrote.[2]

If Walt Disney was still alive, he'd probably vacation at Six Flags.

The most recent controversy has centered around the company's decision to oppose an initiative by Florida Governor Ron DeSantis to ban schools from sexually grooming children. The state's new laws forbid teachers from educating their children about things best left to mommy and daddy. Or the family pastor.

But Disney executives don't believe parents should have a say in their child's education. They also believe that four-year-olds should be exposed to sex education lessons.

But now they've gone even further. Disney says they plan to infuse all of their programming with LGBT narratives. And their mission is far from covert. Disney owns ABC television. They spew this perversion into your home twenty-four hours a day.

Recently, *Good Morning America* broadcast a live drag show performance—featuring a young boy in makeup, a dress, and high heels. The child literally gyrated on the floor as grown adults cheered.

This did not happen in a seedy nightclub. It happened on national television.

Franklin Graham, the president of the Billy Graham Evangelistic Association, called out Disney's blatant attack on family values.

"The morals of the corporate leadership of Disney today are in the gutter, and they want to redefine family counter to

---

2 Often uncommon (@oftenuncommon), "Walt is rolling over in his grave," Tweet, July 18, 2022, https://twitter.com/oftenuncommon/status/1549092004579131393?s=20&t=aNcrhtliWKRH9z7lFXkbjA.

God's original design and flaunt sin," Graham wrote on his Twitter page.[3]

"LGBTQ activists are using corporations to force their agenda on the public, and companies may want to take another look at what they are allowing to happen," he added. "Disney has gone too far."

Graham predicted that Disney will suffer significant backlash from parents as well as lawmakers.

"The people of Florida have revolted, and it's going to cost Disney big time. Disney had a special tax status in the state which they benefited from in a huge way—but because they came out against the parents of Florida, the governor and legislators have revoked that status," he said.

What has happened at Disney is moral failure, the renowned evangelist said.

"Walt Disney had a vision for wholesome family entertainment. He was committed to the family," he said.

In the old days, the predators drove around in white vans. Nowadays, they wear mouse ears.

Former Arkansas governor Mike Huckabee left little to the imagination during a recent interview on my radio show.

"I don't think we need to be teaching four- and five-year-olds the difference between the cowboy position and the missionary position," Huckabee said. "I mean, I just don't think that that's where four- and five-year-olds need to be instructed. So, this is not about a particular lifestyle. This is simply about the greater

---

3 Jimmy McCloskey, "Evangelical Pastor Franklin Graham Says Disney's 'Morals Are in the Gutter' and Backs DeSantis," *Daily Mail*, April 24, 2022, https://www.dailymail.co.uk/news/article-10749431/Evangelical-Pastor-Franklin-Graham-says-Disneys-morals-gutter-backs-DeSantis.html

issue of whether sexuality and the teaching of it belongs in the mind of a four- or five-year-old."

Never in a million years would I have imagined that Disney would not only go woke, but they would turn into a bunch of creepy perverts.

"Well, Todd, you and I, we're just not woke enough," Huckabee said. "I mean, we kind of grew up in the time when boys were boys and girls were girls, and we knew the difference and we kind of liked the difference. And now we're not supposed to know the difference. And if we do know the difference, we're supposed to keep shut up about it. So it's very confusing, but I'm going to just stick with the old biblical model, male and female. He created them and kind of figure out that maybe that's where we should stay."

DISNEY WEEDING OUT CHRISTIAN STAFFERS

A former Walt Disney World employee claims the company doesn't want Christians in their parks or on their payroll.

In an interview with Fox News, Barbara Andreas, who was let go in March of 2022, said, "We've been very vocal that it feels like Disney is getting closer and closer to not wanting Christians there. Not on their parks, not on their payroll."[4]

This comes after two other former Disney employees were fired after giving religious exemptions for the vaccine; they are now suing the company for religious discrimination.

Barbara Andreas says she was called out by a general manager, "made to feel like a bad person, a bad leader, and totally singled out."

---

4 Kyle Rossiter, "Disney Doesn't Want Christians in their Parks, Says Ex-Employee," KWAM, July 13, 2022, https://mighty990.com/disney-doesnt-want-christians-in-their-parks-says-ex-employee/.

Both employees claim to have reached out multiple times about the status of their exemptions but were ignored by their higher-ups at Disney. When Stephen Cribb, the other employee, asked to have an attorney present, they allegedly refused further conversations regarding his exemption.

Carroll Sanders, the attorney representing them, "spent a great deal of time reaching out" as well and was met with similar silence before filing the lawsuit. He continued to say they have "at least a dozen more plaintiffs in the pipeline" meaning the lawsuit could grow to a larger problem for Disney.

"We want to be valued; we want to be accepted.... Disney just thinks they are above the law," said Andreas.

Disney's decision to jump into the culture wars has caused significant debate with the nation's Christian community. But I sincerely doubt it will lead to any real corporate change.

Christians are addicted to Disney. They claim to oppose the company's anti-Christian, anti-family agenda, but most have decided it was not enough to change their vacation plans.

Just look at how the Southern Baptist Convention handled Disney. The nation's largest Protestant denomination literally embraced Disney during its recent convention in California.

They held the national convention in Anaheim during the middle of the LGBT battle, and instead of encouraging Baptists to boycott, they actually embraced Disney. What sort of messages does it send to Christians when Southern Baptist leaders are partying at the Magic Kingdom?

DISNEY REMOVES "ZIP-A-DEE-DOO-DAH"

Disney has removed a beloved song from its daily parade at Disneyland, sanitizing its theme parks of anything that might trigger the woke Left.

"Zip-a-Dee-Doo-Dah," a song that has brought countless joy to millions of Americans, has been given the heave-ho after critics said it was racist.

It was featured prominently in the 1946 classic, *Song of the South*. The film is set in the post–Civil War South and explores the friendship between a white boy and an elderly black man.

Of course, there's nothing remotely racist about *Song of the South* or "Zip-a-Dee-Doo-Dah."

The song won an Academy Award for best original song. And James Baskett, the star of the film, became the first black man to win an Oscar. It seems to me we should be celebrating the film, not erasing it.

Disney CEO Bob Iger has stated that *Song of the South* is "just not appropriate in today's world."

Disney World also dismantled Splash Mountain because the ride was based on characters from the movie.

Disney has yet to explain how the lyrics of "Zip-a-Dee-Doo-Dah" and Splash Mountain are racist.

The songwriters were known for writing songs that included nonsensical words: "Bibbidi-Bobbidi-Boo" from Cinderella and "Supercalifragilisticexpialidocious" from Mary Poppins.

Making up words was their trademark. It was gibberish—much like the arguments from the cancel culture mob.

A feel-good song now banished to the cancel culture's dustbin of history.

If only the bluebird of happiness would pay a visit to the cars of those woke busybodies.

My, oh my, what a wonderful day that would be.

DISNEY BANS HIGH SCHOOL MARCHING BAND

Woke Disney World is no longer the happiest place on Earth.

In 2022, theme park executives told a high school marching band they would not be allowed to march in a parade—just hours before show time.

It seems the folks who run Disney took offense at Venice High School's mascot—the Indians. School leaders were told to cover up the Native American logo and change the name of their band.

Disney had originally approved the band's performance during the November 2022 parade but walked back its offer after a change in policy, according to a letter sent to parents by Principal Zoltan Kerestely.

"Disney has stated that they are not allowing any depiction of Native Americans to be portrayed during events," Kerestely wrote.

Instead of bowing down to the woke mob, the high school decided to stand its ground.

"We are very proud of the Venice High School Band and stand behind our decision to not participate during the Disney event," the school district said in a statement to television station WTSP.[5] "Our students deserve to be honored and celebrated without having to change their school name or alter the school

5 Andrea Chu, "Venice High Band Won't Perform at Disney over Native American Mascot," WTSP Tampa Bay, November 7, 2022, https://www.wtsp.com/article/news/local/sarasotacounty/venice-band-disney-performance-indian-native-american-mascot/67-aaf1235d-4dce-407e-8935-d34eb3a66dd3.

logo. We will continue to look for other opportunities where our students can be accepted and acknowledged for their superior musical ability."

The school boldly pleaded its case, but Disney held firm. The kids were allowed to hang out in the park, but they were booted from the parade.

Carl Brown, the former president of the boosters and parent of a marching band student, was unhappy with the situation.

"It is such a disgraceful thing that they had to do in order to march and perform for their customers," Brown told MySunCoast.com.[6] "They are asking our kids to cover a logo that they're all proud of."

Kudos to Venice High School for refusing to bow down to Woke Disney World.

The drum beats of the culture war thunder across the nation, but it's nice to know the Venice High School Indians march to the beat of a different drum.

DISNEY PROMOTES SATANIC CARTOON FOR KIDS

What in the name of Tinker Bell is happening at Disney?

They ran a commercial during a LSU–Florida State game promoting a new animated comedy series called *Little Demon.*

It's about Satan and the Antichrist.

"Thirteen years after being impregnated by Satan, a reluctant mother, Laura, and her Antichrist daughter, Chrissy, attempt to live an ordinary life in Delaware, but are constantly thwarted

---

6 ABC7 Staff, "Venice High School Will No Longer Perform at Disney World," My Suncoast ABC7, November 4, 2022, https://www.mysuncoast.com/2022/11/05/venice-highschool-will-no-longer-perform-disney-world/.

by monstrous forces, including Satan, who yearns for custody of his daughter's soul." Executive producer Aubrey Plaza, the actress who voices Laura, makes no apologies for the satanic content. She said in an interview, "I love that we are normalizing paganism. Laura is a pagan. She's a witch. She's jacked."

The cartoon airs on FX and FXX—channels owned and operated by The Walt Disney Company.

Congressman Mike Johnson, the Republican from Louisiana, brought national attention to the show. "They chose to run this ad during the second quarter as a trailer for this, I mean, truly demonic, I mean, by design, a demonic sitcom cartoon. And I just was so, I was so disturbed by it. And I just felt like people needed to know," said Johnson on my radio show.

"Our job as parents is to guard the hearts and minds of our kids," he wrote. "This culture has become alarmingly dark and desensitized and this is not a game. Disney and FX have decided to embrace and market what is clearly evil."

Sadly, Disney is no longer about Donald Duck or Goofy or the Mickey Mouse Club.

The happiest place on Earth has become a dangerous force for evil in the culture, advancing a radical sex and gender agenda while embracing the occult.

Walt Disney World replaced Prince Charming with the Prince of Darkness.

WHY DOES MINNIE MOUSE LOOK LIKE A MAN?

Disney's beloved Minnie Mouse is getting a makeover. Replacing her iconic red, polka-dot dress with a gender-neutral pantsuit.

Minnie Mouse is apparently getting fashion advice from Hillary Clinton.

News of the makeover came just days after the makers of M&M's announced they, too, were making their candies less feminine, more masculine.

The sex and gender revolutionaries prefer that the candy that melts in your mouth, not in your hands, parades around in Birkenstocks instead of stilettos.

Disney says they wanted to put Minnie in pants as a symbol of progress for a new generation of women.

So the next time you visit Disney World, don't be surprised if you see a nonbinary M&M wearing sensible shoes cavorting with a gender-neutral mouse wearing trousers.

I'm just glad Walt Disney's not alive to see what the diversity crowd has done to his beloved cartoon world.

Cruella de Woke.

DISNEY CANCELS CHRISTMAS

Mickey's Very Merry Christmas Party, an extremely popular yuletide tradition, is going to be rebranded. Instead, the Magic Kingdom will host a nighttime secular holiday show.

The new "don't call it Christmas" event is called "Disney Very Merriest After Hours"—a generic holiday-themed celebration.

Whoever came up with that idea deserves a lump of coal in their Christmas stocking.

Disney did not provide an explanation for the change, but in recent days, the woke imagineers at the Magic Kingdom have made national headlines by culturally cleansing many popular rides.

Among the "offensive rides" that have been updated are Pirates of the Caribbean ride and, as I previously mentioned, Splash Mountain—a ride inspired by *Song of the South*. They also updated the Jungle Cruise over concerns about the depictions of natives.

There was even controversy surrounding Prince Charming's life-saving kiss that awakened Snow White from her slumber. The #MeToo crowd took issue with the "unwelcomed" smooch.

Disney also eliminated the words "ladies and gentlemen" and "boys and girls" from recorded greetings at its theme parks, as I mentioned earlier in Chapter 17.

In April 2021, Disney announced it was adding "Inclusion" as a key component of its customer service. "We want our guests to see their own backgrounds and traditions reflected in the stories, experiences and products they encounter in their interactions with Disney," the company said.[7]

The original introduction included, "Good evening, ladies and Gentlemen, boys and girls, dreamers of all ages." Now, the greeting is, "Good evening, dreamers of all ages."

And how can we forget that Disney wanted its white staffers to complete a "white privilege" training workshop?[8] What in the name of Jiminy Cricket is going on?

Disney fans are beyond outraged over the Cancel Christmas news, accusing the Magic Kingdom of appeasing critics.

---

7 Greg Cannella, "Disney Removes 'Ladies and Gentlemen, Boys and Girls' Greeting from Magic Kingdom Fireworks Show," CBS News, July 2, 2021, https://www.cbsnews.com/news/disney-removes-ladies-and-gentlemen-boys-and-girls-magic-kingdom-fireworks/.

8 SMG News Wire, "Disney Sounds like It's Becoming the Most Racist Place on Earth," Todd Starnes, May 11, 2021, https://www.toddstarnes.com/values/starnes-disney-sounds-like-its-becoming-the-most-racist-place-on-earth/.

"We can only believe that Disney is continuing to follow the stupidity already shown in changing cast costumes so as not to offend, or erasing all gender in their traditional welcome and greeting that included both boys and girls," one angry fan wrote on Facebook. "Disney, I have been your biggest Mouseketeer fan for 46 years but you are losing many of us who actually keep your business going while you try to appeal to critics and the habitually offended. Get it together or just shut down completely, because you will NEVER make those kinds of people happy."

Another Mouseketeer noted, "I'm all for equality and respecting people's differences, but now they're taking away cherished traditions from the mainstream in the name of extreme political correctness."

It is not exactly clear what's going to happen during Disney World's After Hours show. Will there be Christmas trees? What about wreaths or a Nativity scene? How about the beloved candlelight processional?

We simply do not know the extent of the cultural cleansing of Disney's "holiday" celebration, but don't be surprised if it lands somebody on Santa's naughty list.

DISNEY TO ADD WARNING LABELS TO *PETER PAN, DUMBO*

Children are going to have a much harder time watching Disney classics like *Peter Pan*, *Dumbo*, and *Swiss Family Robinson*.

Disney says they are adding kid filters and warning labels to all those classic movies—*The Aristocats* too.[9]

---

9 Nexstar Media Wire, "Negative Stereotypes in 'Dumbo,' 'Peter Pan' Lead to Movies Removed from Children's Profiles on Disney+," Fox 59, March 9, 2021, https://fox59.com/news/entertainment/negative-stereotypes-in-dumbo-peter-pan-lead-to-movies-removed-from-childrens-profiles-on-disney/.

There is a full-scale war on American culture by a gang of jihadists who want to turn our history and traditions into a pile of rubble.

Disney says the movies include negative depictions of people and cultures. These changes are part of their effort to create a more inclusive future for Americans.

The problem with *Dumbo* is the song and dance number featuring the elephant and a bunch of black crows. Disney says the scene was an homage to racist minstrel shows.

"The leader of the group in *Dumbo* is Jim Crow, which shares the name of laws that enforced racial segregation in the Southern United States," Disney said in a statement.

Peter Pan and *Swiss Family Robinson* were hit for their negative portrayals of Indians and pirates.

"It shows them speaking in an unintelligible language and repeatedly refers to them as 'redskins,' an offensive term."

As for the pirates?

"The pirates who antagonize the Robinson family are portrayed as a stereotypical foreign menace," Disney said.

As for *The Aristocats*, one of the cats is depicted with slanted eyes and buck teeth.

"The Siamese cat Shun Gon is depicted as a racist caricature of East Asian peoples with exaggerated stereotypical traits such as slanted eyes and buck teeth."

There were some classic films that were spared from Disney's Wonderful World of cultural cleansing—*The Country Bears* and *The Adventures of Tom Sawyer*—shows that portrayed white folks as a bunch of barefoot hillbillies who play banjos. I'm sure that was just an oversight. And if you believe that, welcome to Fantasy Land.

18
DIXIE HAS DONE GONE WOKE

DURING MY EARLY years at Fox News, I had the chance to interview one half of a popular country music duo. I made an offhanded comment about why people love country music—specifically because unlike soy latte-sipping pop stars, country music stars drive pickup trucks, drink sweet tea, own guns, and love America.

While I meant for the comment to be a joke, it really is the gospel truth. For most of its existence, the country music industry has been a standard-bearer of American values, except for a few songs about bar fights and conduct unbecoming of a Baptist in a trailer park.

A few minutes after the interview, my producer came back to my desk with a concerned look on her face. After the interview had concluded, the country music star called back and was not too happy. He told my producer he was angry, and he took great offense at my comments. He accused me of stereotyping country music singers and fans. It turns out this particular country music singer enjoyed sipping soy milk lattes while flouting about Nashville in one of those battery-powered, metrosexual, foreign-made cars.

Little did I know at the time that country music had become infected with a malaise known as culture creep. It's sort of like kudzu. Once it starts growing on something, you can't get rid of it.

And sure enough, ten years after my interview with that leftist crooner, the industry that gave us Hank and Johnny and George had been taken over by fellows squeezed into skinny jeans, reeking of essential oils and dishing about their bromances onstage at the Grand Ole Opry.

Let me put it this way—if Minnie Pearl was in a bar fight with a bunch of those bromance boys at a honky-tonk on Lower Broadway, she'd smack the spray tan right off their moisturized faces.

Billboard magazine blew the lid off the butter beans in 2018 by reporting that the country music industry was more liberal than it let on. Not long after the Dixie Chicks, now known as "The Chicks," were excommunicated in 2003 for their on-stage attacks against President Bush, a group of liberal music executives formed a coalition.

"Fifteen years later, this contrast has never been more apparent," *Billboard* reported. "The past year in Nashville—a city that consistently votes blue—has transformed the town from comfortably silent to one vociferously at odds with the conservative political agenda."[1]

"Liberal used to be a dirty word in country music," the *Tampa Bay Times* declared. "But today, more artists are speaking out on gun control, LGBTQ rights and immigration. And some are stumping for a Democratic wave on Election Day."

In other words, the denim and diamond crowd on Lower Broadway just got woke. The *Times* went so far as to say a blue hue had settled over Music Row. The question is whether coun-

1 Marissa R. Moss, "The Country Music Industry Is More Liberal Than It Lets On: Will More Start To Speak Up?" *Billboard*, June 5, 2018, https://www.billboard.com/music/country/why-liberal-country-music-artists-executives-dont-speak-up-8458774/.

try music fans will follow their favorite musicians to the left side of the stage.

And that brings me to an incident that occurred in 2018 when one of country music's most powerful executives said gun-toting, Bible-clinging fans like former Arkansas governor Mike Huckabee are no longer welcome.

The controversy started when the Country Music Association (CMA) triggered a massive outbreak of microaggressions after they appointed Huckabee to the board of its charitable foundation. Huckabee has been a longtime supporter of music education, so his appointment to a charitable board that supports music programs for young people was a perfect fit.

However, a mob of social justice warriors, led by openly gay country music executive Jason Owen, protested calling Huckabee's appointment "grossly offensive" and "heartbreaking."

"This man has made it clear that my family is not welcome in his America," the owner of Sandbox Entertainment wrote in a letter to the CMA. "And the CMA has opened their arms to him, making him feel welcome and relevant."

Owen, whose roster includes Faith Hill, Little Big Town, Kacey Musgraves, and Midland, threatened to pull out of the CMA Foundation over Huckabee's appointment.

"Huckabee speaks of the sort of things that would suggest my family is morally beneath his and uses language that has a profoundly negative impact upon young people all across this country," he wrote.[2]

---

2 Oliver Willis, "Country Music Fans Force Mike Huckabee out of Charity over His Bigotry," The American Independent, March 1, 2018, https://americanindependent.com/mike-huckabee-charity-country-music-fans/.

For the record, Huckabee is a born-again Southern Baptist preacher who follows the teachings of the Holy Bible. And that includes the Bible's directives on marriage. And I'd also be willing to bet a gallon of sweet tea and a bucket of chicken that a good many country music fans go to church, own a gun, and share the same beliefs as Governor Huckabee. That's why there are more country music songs about God and pickup trucks and honky-tonks instead of Chevy Volts and juice bars.

Owen also objected to the former governor's involvement with the National Rifle Association calling it "harmful and damaging."

"What a shameful choice," he wrote. "I will not participate in any organization that elevates people like this to positions that amplify their sick voices."

Has it really come to this, America? Must we renounce our religious beliefs and bow down to those who will not tolerate tolerance? Does the country music industry really consider their base to be people with "sick voices"?

Less than twenty-four hours later, Huckabee resigned from the CMA Foundation board and wrote an open letter to the industry titled "Hate Wins." The governor permitted me to share his letter in this book, and it's worth reading:

> Dear Board Members:
>
> It appears that I will make history as having the shortest tenure in the history of the CMA Foundation Board. I genuinely regret that some in the industry were so outraged by my appointment that they bullied the CMA and the Foundation with economic threats and vowed to

withhold support for the programs for students if I remained. I had NO idea I was that influential! I'm somewhat flattered to be of such consequence when all I thought I was doing was voluntarily serving on a non-profit board without pay in order to continue my decades of advocacy for the arts and especially music.

The message here is "Hate Wins." Bullies succeeded in making it untenable to have "someone like me" involved. I would imagine however that many of the people who buy tickets and music are not that "unlike me."

I hereby tender my resignation effective immediately. I hope this will end the unnecessary distraction and deterrent to the core mission of the Foundation which is to help kids acquire musical instruments and have an opportunity to participate in music programs as students.

Since I will not be able to continue in what I had hoped to be useful service in this endeavor, I wanted to at least put some things on the record. I have no expectation that it will change the irrational vitriol directed toward you or me for my religious or political views that necessitated my abrupt departure, but I want you to know what you would never know by reading intolerant and vicious statements on the internet about who I am or what led me to want to be a part of your efforts to empower kids with the gift of music. So please bear with me.

Music changed my life. I grew up dirt poor in south Arkansas. No male upstream from me in my entire family ever even graduated from high school. I had no reason to believe that my life would consist of anything but scratching out a meager living and hoping to pay rent in a house I would never own just as generations before me had done.

Music changed that. The gift of an electric guitar by my parents when I was 11 put in my hands a future. It took them a year to pay for the $99 guitar they bought from the J. C. Penney catalog. Granted, I was never good enough to make a full-time living at music, but the confidence I gained by playing, being in front of people, and competing against myself and the low expectations I grew up with was transformative.

No need to recite my entire history, but I was especially baffled that I was accused of not being supportive of public education. I am the PRODUCT of public education. As Governor my own children were the first children of a Governor in 50 years to have their entire education grades 1-12 in the PUBLIC schools of Arkansas. I fought to give teachers the largest pay raise in state history. I successfully led the effort to allow teachers to retire with full benefits after 28 years of service after my two Democrat predecessors vetoed the same bill. I personally shepherded through legislation that mandated both music AND arts programs for EVERY student in grades 1-12 and taught by fully certified teachers. We were one of the only states to have ever done that.

I was Chairman for 2 years of the Education Commission of the States, comprised of all 50 Governors, education leaders in the Senate and House from all 50 state legislatures, and the state education chief for each of the 50 states. My chosen theme and agenda for those two years was music education for every child. I launched an initiative "Play it Again, Arkansas" that promoted donation of musical instruments that would be professionally refurbished and provided to students whose parents couldn't afford the rent or purchase of an instrument allowing them to be in the school band. I traveled repeatedly to DC with the NAMM Foundation to advocate for music education and have worked with them for several years to urge states to mandate music and arts education. Now someone who has never met me threatens to wreck valuable programs of the CMA Foundation because of a personal contempt for my faith and politics. I am willing to get out of the way for the sake of the students the Foundation will hopefully help.

If the industry doesn't want people of faith or who hold conservative and traditional political views to buy tickets and music, they should be forthcoming and say it. Surely neither the artists or the business people of the industry want that.

Until recently, the arts was the one place America could set aside political, geographical, racial, religious, and economic barriers and come together. If the arts community becomes part of the polarization instead of bridging communities and people over the power of civil norms as reflected in the arts, then we as a civilization may not be long for this earth.

All of us have deep passions about our beliefs. I do about mine. But I hate no one. I wish upon NO ONE the loss of life or livelihood because that person sees things differently than me.

I hope that the music and entertainment industry will become more tolerant and inclusive and recognize that a true love for kids having access to the arts is more important than a dislike for someone or a group of people because of who they are or what they believe.

My sincere thanks to the CMA Foundation for believing I had something to contribute. I regret that my presence caused controversy and threats to vital support for deserving kids. Kids wanting

> to learn music shouldn't be the victims of adults who demand that only certain people can be in the room or be heard.
>
> I wish you nothing but good will and success at reaching students across America who need music as much as I did. At the end of the day, I'm not worth the fight, but the kids are. Never stop fighting for THEM!
>
> Sincerely,
> Mike Huckabee

Governor Huckabee was a guest on my radio program the day after he mailed the letter. He was quick to point out that he harbored no ill will toward the Country Music Association Foundation.

"I'm not mad at them. I feel sad that we are in a place in our country—the last place where people could get together and find common ground for civilized behavior, which was the arts, is now becoming itself a polarized place in society, and that's just tragic," the governor said.

And the culprits are people like Jason Owen who scream about tolerance while privately trying to destroy anyone who does not conform to his personal moral code. Again, Governor Huckabee was deemed unfit because of his Christian convictions regarding marriage and because of his membership in the National Rifle Association.

"What is inclusion if inclusion only means people who have a very strong, and very far left-of-center point of view? That's not inclusion," the governor told me. "When people on the left say love, they mean hate. When they say tolerant, they mean intolerant. When they say diversity, what they really mean is conformity."

In reality, an overwhelming number of Americans and country music fans share the governor's moral code, not Jason Owen's. So why didn't Governor Huckabee demand that Owen be removed from his position on the CMA Foundation? It's because the governor is a tolerant man, and he understood that the foundation is not about gay marriage or gun control. The foundation is about music education.

Folks, I'd be lying if I said I was not concerned about Governor Huckabee's public flogging. As difficult as it may be, we have to ask whether the country music industry has been overrun by a bunch of anti-Christian, gun-hating bullies.

I certainly hope that is not the case, but one thing is mighty clear—we're not in Kornfield Kounty anymore, *Hee Haw* fans. And as the following dispatches from the front lines of the culture war will demonstrate, there is a full-scale cultural cleansing underway in the Southern states.

OLE MISS BANS THE DIXIE FIGHT SONG

The University of Mississippi has officially dumped "Dixie" so they can be more inclusive. I fear old times there will soon be forgotten, folks.

"The newly expanded and renovated Vaught-Hemingway Stadium will further highlight our best traditions and create new ones that give the Ole Miss Rebels the best home field advantage in college football," the university announced.

"Dixie" was first played by the Ole Miss band around 1948, *Mississippi Today* reports.[3]

"Because the Pride of the South is such a large part of our overall experience and tradition, the Athletics Department asked them to create a new and modern pregame show that does not include Dixie and is more inclusive for all fans," the university declared.

More inclusive, eh?

Perhaps they could consult with Beyonce or Jay-Z. I'm certain the university will find some inspiration from her 2016 Super Bowl halftime performance.

It's only a matter of time before Ole Miss replaces fried catfish and sweet tea with fermented soy sandwiches and beverages made from lawn clippings—all for the sake of inclusivity.

Allen Coon, a student government leader, was thrilled with the university's decision.

"It's an important step forward for our university as we attempt to reconcile and understand our relationship with our Old South past," Coon told the *Commercial Appeal*.[4] "Ending the use of 'Dixie' promotes inclusivity and makes room for traditions that all UM students can connect with."

In its quest to be politically correct, I wonder if Ole Miss will also ban various genres of music that include offensive lyrics about women? And what about modern-day music that employs the use of a certain racial epithet? Would Ole Miss consider rap and hip-hop taboo too? It's doubtful.

---

3 Adam Ganucheau, "For Ole Miss Sports, 'Dixie' Is Dead," Mississippi Today, August 19, 2016, https://mississippitoday.org/2016/08/19/for-ole-miss-sports-dixie-is-dead/.

4 Ron Maxey, "Ole Miss to Stop Playing Dixie at Football Games This Fall," Commercial Appeal, August 19, 2016, https://archive.commercialappeal.com/mobile-topstories/ole-miss-to-stop-playing-dixie-at-football-games-this-fall-3a722e9d-dbe3-5ccc-e053-0100007fc761-390725801.html/.

Ole Miss has been shedding its Southern heritage for quite some time now. Confederate flags have been effectively banned since 1997, reports *Mississippi Today*. Last year, they banned the Mississippi state flag.

Colonel Rebel, the school's mascot, was sidelined from games in 2003 because critics said he looked too much like a white plantation owner. He was replaced by a black bear. And in 2009, they told the band to stop playing "From Dixie with Love," in part because fans were yelling, "The South will rise again," during the song.

A reader of the *Oxford Eagle*, the official newspaper of record, summed up the sentiment of many Mississippians.

"Ole Miss is despicable for doing this," the gentleman wrote. "The university keeps bowing before the boot of political correctness."

And it ain't over, folks. It would be foolish to think the progressive academic elites have concluded their quest to eradicate Southern culture and traditions. It won't be long before someone mounts a campaign to remove the word "rebel" from the school's athletic teams.

The only question is whether that happens before or after one of those perpetually offended, liberal snowflakes files a federal lawsuit demanding the university change its name.

I can already imagine the headlines:

- "Students Say 'Ole Miss' Causes Microaggressions"
- "Safe Spaces Overrun by Victims of 'Ole Miss' White Privilege"
- "President Ocasio-Cortez Signs Executive Order Renaming 'Ole Miss' the University of Obama"

Come to think of it, that last headline may not be all that far-fetched.

Meanwhile, progressive liberals continue to bulldoze across the Southern states burning, torching, and tearing down every vestige and cultural tradition of the Deep South much like General Sherman did during the Civil War. Look away Dixieland—just look away.

NORTH CAROLINA TOWN DETERMINES "DIXIE" IS OFFENSIVE

Cultural progressives in Winston-Salem, North Carolina, want to change the name of the Dixie Classic Fair.

They say the word "Dixie" is offensive.

Councilman James Taylor told FOX8 that some folks find the word "offensive," and some folks are "angry" with the name. He said that as a progressive city, they need a name that "everyone can appreciate."[5]

The fair is just the latest victim of a cultural cleansing of the Southern states by angry liberals wound up tighter than a pair of Daisy Dukes.

They're trying to dig up a dead Confederate general in Memphis. They want to sand blast Robert E. Lee's face off the side of Stone Mountain, Georgia. And Lord only knows what they want to do with Aunt Jemima and Uncle Ben.

The Dixie Classic Fair has been around since the 1950s—and nobody around town seems to be all that irate, according to FOX8. They said their reporters could not find a single person who took offense at the name.

---

5 Michael Hennessey, "'Dixie Classic Fair' Name in Question, Council Member Says Some Find It 'Offensive,'" FOX8, August 11, 2015, https://myfox8.com/news/dixie-classic-fair-name-in-question-council-member-says-some-find-it-offensive/.

"I thought it was ridiculous," resident Dina Nelson told the television station. "I mean, there's no reason to change the name of the Dixie Classic Fair. I mean, it's a Southern name—but there's nothing racist about it."

If the cultural cleansers succeed in their quest to ban the word "Dixie," don't be surprised if they start banning Dixie Cups or Winn-Dixie.

I really hope they don't try to ban Dixie Cups, folks. How else would you be able to drink Dixie Beer with Hollywood star Dixie Carter?

GONE WITH THE WIND IS GONE WITH THE WIND

Common sense has even gone with the wind in my hometown of Memphis, Tennessee.[6]

The famed Orpheum Theatre has announced it will no longer show summertime screenings of *Gone with the Wind*, ending a thirty-four-year Mid-South tradition. The Orpheum Theatre Group told me they made the decision to exclude the classic film from its 2018 summer movie series over "specific inquiries from patrons."

"As an organization whose stated mission is to 'entertain, educate and enlighten the communities it serves', the Orpheum cannot show a film that is insensitive to a large segment of its local population," the theatre company announced in a statement.[7]

---

6 Todd Starnes, "Common Sense Is Gone with the Wind in Memphis," Todd Starnes, August 28, 2017, https://www.toddstarnes.com/uncategorized/common-sense-is-gone-with-the-wind-in-memphis/.

7 John Beifuss, "'Gone with the Wind' Is Gone – from Memphis Theater After 34 Years," Commercial Appeal, August 25, 2017, https://www.commercialappeal.com/story/news/2017/08/25/gone-wind-gone-orpheum/601949001/.

Television station WREG noted in its coverage that the African-American population of Memphis is about 64 percent.

"While title selections for the series are typically made in the spring of each year, the Orpheum has made this determination early in response to specific inquiries from patrons," the statement read.

It's bad enough that Memphis leaders dug up the dead body of Confederate General Nathan Bedford Forrest from a local park, but now they want to ban Prissy and Scarlett and Rhett and Aunt Pittypat. This cultural cleansing of my hometown has gone too far.

Brett Batterson, the president of the Orpheum Theatre Group, told the *Commercial Appeal* the decision was made before the violence in Charlottesville, Virginia.

"This is about the Orpheum wanting to be inclusive and welcoming to all of Memphis," he told the newspaper.

Frankly, Mr. Batterson, I don't give a damn.

Sadly, I predicted that it would be only a matter of time before the culture jihadists targeted Tara.

And now our beloved film is gone with the wind—done in by a bunch of meddling, no-account thespian carpetbaggers (to be fair, I am not sure where Mr. Batterson's people are from, but I don't think they're from around the Mid-South).

Many Memphians must be wondering what has come over this here town. To borrow a phrase from *Gone with the Wind*, liberals have come over it. Same as they've come over all of us.

But there's no use crying in our sweet tea, Southerners. We must stand up to the scourge of the intolerant liberals. We must stand up and fight. In the words of Scarlett O'Hara, as God is my witness—we're not gonna let them lick us.

DIGGING UP DEAD CONFEDERATE WAR HEROES

For the past several years, progressives have been waging a culture jihad across the nation. They've been bulldozing our history much like the Islamic Radicals have been doing in Iraq. Sadly, my hometown has suffered a similar fate.[8]

While most of the good citizens of Memphis were attending Wednesday night church services, the mayor and city council were busy finalizing a despicable plot to bypass the law and desecrate a Civil War gravesite.

In October 2017, the Tennessee Historical Commission refused to allow city leaders to remove statues of Nathan Bedford Forrest and Jefferson Davis from two city parks. The city initiated mediation with the state, but that, too, was unsuccessful.

Instead of following the ruling, the mayor and the city council concocted a nefarious plan to disobey the law and take down the statues in the dark of night.

The city council voted in the early afternoon to sell two public parks to a newly formed nonprofit group chaired by a county commissioner. (Anybody smell a rat?)

The two parks—both prized pieces of real estate—were sold for $1,000 each. What kind of a shady real estate deal is that?

While the city council was voting, heavy machinery and an army of police officers were being dispatched to both parks. Did the nonprofit pick up the tab for the police officers and the heavy machinery? Or were taxpayers forced to foot the bill?

---

8 Todd Starnes, "Memphis Mayor Wages Jihad on American History," Todd Starnes, December 21, 2017, https://www.toddstarnes.com/values/memphis-mayor-wages-jihad-american-history/.

"The law allows a private entity to remove items such as statues from its own land," Mayor Jim Strickland told bewildered citizens.

After the city council passed the sham real estate deal, the cowardly mayor issued a notice on social media.

"Health Science Park and Memphis Park have been sold," the mayor declared. "Operations on those sites tonight are being conducted by a private entity and are compliant with state law."

Within a matter of hours both statues were removed—in the darkness of night.

"The City made a decision to willfully violate state law and remove the statues of Forrest and Davis," said Thomas Strain of the Sons of Confederate Veterans. "This is a direct violation of state law and we must allow the state to pursue this case in a lawful manner."

James Patterson, the commander of the Tennessee division of the Sons of Confederate Veterans, called it a "well-organized, behind the scenes plan by the city."

"They are willfully violating the Heritage Preservation Act. The City has broken state law," Patterson said.

Beyond that, the bodies of Nathan Bedford Forrest and his wife are buried in one of the parks. Therefore, it was my contention that the mayor and city council are also guilty of desecration.

My fury had nothing to do with the monuments or the memorials. It had nothing to do with selling off prime real estate at a bargain-basement price. My fury had to do with the flagrant disregard of the law.

Mayor Jim Strickland and the Memphis City Council flouted that law. They violated their oath of office, and they desecrated a gravesite.

At the time, I urged the governor and the state legislature to launch an immediate investigation of the corruption that has infested Memphis City Hall. The law demanded it. And I said on my radio program that I looked forward to the day when Mayor Jim Strickland and members of the city council were removed from office and hauled out of City Hall in handcuffs.

The mayor did not take kindly to my remarks—and he took me to task in the local media. He called me a liar. I reckon the mayor must have his own version of the truth—like Oprah.

THE DAY DOLLY PARTON GOT STAMPEDED

Dolly Parton's famous "Dixie Stampede" just got trampled by a politically correct mob. The popular dinner show with locations in Pigeon Forge, Tennessee, and Branson, Missouri, will now be called, "Dolly Parton's Stampede."

For nearly thirty years, the Dixie Stampede has been a family-friendly dinner show attraction—featuring great food and expert horsemanship—steeped in Civil War history. The Starnes family has attended on numerous occasions (we sat on the Southern side).

It's unclear what, specifically, Miss Dolly will be stampeding in the culturally-cleansed revision. And it's also not clear why the sudden name change (but I have a suspicion).

"Our shows currently are identified by where they are located," Miss Dolly said in a press statement. "Some examples are Smoky Mountain Adventures or Dixie Stampede. We also recognize that attitudes change and feel that by streamlining the names of our shows, it will remove any confusion or concerns about our shows and will help our efforts to expand into new cities."

A few years back, *Slate* sent a Yankee reporter to Pigeon Forge to write a scathing review of the Dixie Stampede described as the "Lost Cause of the Confederacy meets Cirque du Soleil."

The writer went on to call the show a "lily-white extravaganza" that celebrates the "Old South." Again, Miss Dolly did not say what influenced the decision to culturally cleanse the Dixie Stampede—but others share my thoughts.

"Well, like everybody else, I love Dolly, and I love all that she's done for our community, which is her community, and I'm disappointed that they're yielding to political correctness," Knox County Mayor Tim Burchett told the *Knoxville News Sentinel*. "What's next? Are we going to change the name of Dixie cups and the Dixie sugar company?"[9] He has a good point.

THE WAR ON THE SOUTHERN DRAWL

As you know, I'm a son of the South. And even though I've lived in New York City for the past decade, I still take my tea sweet, my chicken fried, and my biscuits buttered. I'm proud to call myself a gun-toting, Bible-clinging Tennessee Volunteer.

So you can imagine my befuddlement when I learned the Oak Ridge National Laboratory wanted to crack down on workers who have Southern accents by holding a "Southern Accent Reduction" course.

In other words, them government folks want to learn us rednecks how to talk right. Bless their hearts.

---

9 Maggie Jones, "Dolly Parton's Dixie Stampede Gets Name Change, Now Called Stampede," Knox News, January 9, 2018, https://www.knoxnews.com/story/entertainment/2018/01/09/dolly-partons-dixie-stampede-gets-name-change-now-called-stampede/1017388001/.

The *Knoxville News Sentinel* reports the government-managed facility wanted to bring in a "nationally certified speech pathologist and accent reduction trainer."

"Feel confident in a meeting when you need to speak with a more neutral American accent, and be remembered for what you say and not how you say it," read a notice that was sent to workers.[10]

A neutral American accent? That sounds about as appealing as a fermented soy sandwich with a side of bean curd.

Needless to say, Oak Ridge's edict stirred up a mess of trouble, and they eventually called off the class.

"Given the way that it came across, they decided to cancel it," lab spokesman David Keim told the newspaper.

So what's wrong with a Southern drawl?

Scientific American reported in 2012 that some Americans say a Southern accent sounds "ignorant."

"Studies have shown that whether you are from the North or South, a Southern twang pegs the speaker as comparatively dim-witted, but also likely to be a nicer person than folks who speak like a Yankee," the publication reported.[11]

Folks, if Southern-fried stereotypes like that don't grip your grits, I don't know what will. For the record, Southerners do not talk funny. We just like to savor our vowels—let them linger for a bit.

---

10 Alan Greenblatt, "Y'all Keep Talking: Lab Scratches 'Southern Accent Reduction' Course," NPR, July 29, 2014, https://www.npr.org/sections/thetwo-way/2014/07/29/336364371/yall-keep-talking-lab-scratches-southern-accent-reduction-course.

11 R. Douglas Fields, "Why Does a Southern Drawl Sound Uneducated to Some?" *Scientific American*, December 7, 2012, https://blogs.scientificamerican.com/guest-blog/why-does-a-southern-drawl-sound-uneducated-to-some/.

I'm beginning to wonder if this attack on Southern diction is part of a much larger crusade to eradicate our way of life—our traditions. One liberal reader took me to task for mentioning that Tennesseans enjoy eating catfish and hush puppies. The reader accused me of stereotyping. I tried to explain to the guy that I happened to be from Tennessee, and I enjoy eating both fried catfish and hush puppies. It's not stereotyping. It's just good eatin'.

I mentioned that encounter on my Facebook page, and soon my newsfeed lit up with irate readers. A fan from southern New York mentioned that he loved catfish. Some church ladies from Alabama said they eat their fish with a side of white beans. And a guy from Dallas reminded everyone that the catfish are actually bigger in Texas.

Why, I even received correspondence from someone living among the liberals of the Pacific Northwest. He said they've been known to throw down with some deep fried halibut and cornbread.

The general consensus among my readers and radio listeners is that folks who don't like the Southern way of life should just mind their own business. That being said, it's probably a good thing I didn't mention that I enjoy hoe cakes too.

I have noticed, though, that Southern traditions are under assault. They're serving barbecue tofu in Asheville and tuna tartare at the Opryland Hotel. Just the other day, I was in Texas and ordered a glass of sweet tea and a buttermilk biscuit. The waitress told me they stopped serving sweet tea—and the only bread product they had was something called a bran muffin with flax seed. I'm sure it's quite tasty—if you happen to be a constipated bird.

Friends, the South is suffering from something called culture creep, and it's spreading across Dixie like kudzu. One day, your neighborhood diner is serving unsweetened tea—and the next day, your neighborhood is home to a yoga shop, a Prius dealership, and a farm-to-table restaurant serving eggs delivered by an Amish midwife.

I'm a bit disappointed Oak Ridge decided to cancel the class, though. I was looking forward to watching the feds teach a bunch of good ole boys how to converse like federal government bureaucrats.

It's not every day you get to see somebody talk out their wazoo.

TWO-SLICE HILLY

There is a bipartisan rule in the Deep South: you never question the authenticity of a Southern woman's homemade pecan pie. Ever.

You can debate the merits of cornbread dressing versus chestnut stuffing. You can argue over roasting the turkey instead of deep frying the turkey. You can even thumb your nose at Aunt Maylene's prized ambrosia.

But it is considered ill-mannered and uncouth to suggest a Southern woman would sully the sanctity of the Thanksgiving Day table with a store-bought pecan pie. And that brings me to one of the most absurd conspiracy theories to hit the Trump administration.

White House Press Secretary Sarah Sanders, a daughter of the great state of Arkansas, had been doing some baking—and she posted a picture of her culinary masterpiece on Twitter.

"I don't cook much these days, but managed this Chocolate Pecan Pie for Thanksgiving at the family farm," she wrote.

The delicious pie stirred the suspicions of CNN political analyst April Ryan, who all but accused the White House press secretary of faking the pie.

"Show it to us on a table," Ms. Ryan tweeted.

For the sake of full disclosure, Ms. Ryan blocked me on Twitter—so I'm relying on images of her Tweets from my Fox News colleagues.

"I am not trying to be funny but folks are already saying #piegate and #fakepie. Show it to us on the table with folks eating it and a pic of you cooking it. I am getting the biggest laugh out of this. I am thankful for this laugh on Black Friday," Ryan tweeted.[12]

Ms. Ryan has some nerve questioning the authenticity of a Southern woman's homemade pecan pie. She may as well have accused Ms. Sanders of bringing a bucket of store-bought chicken to the Wednesday Night Church Fellowship Supper. So, I reached out to Ms. Sanders to get to the bottom of the pie dish.

"Of course I made the pie," Sanders told me. "I make it for every holiday family gathering and have for years."

A source close to the Sanders and Huckabee families confirmed to me the authenticity and the tastiness of the pecan pies.

Ms. Sanders was using a recipe handed down to her by her mother and her grandmother.

"I also used to make them for my neighbors on my street at Christmas every year," Sanders said.

---

12 Kathleen Joyce, "Sarah Sanders embroiled in pecan pie debate with White House reporter," Fox News, November 25, 2017, https://www.foxnews.com/politics/sarah-sanders-embroiled-in-pecan-pie-debate-with-white-house-reporter.

In spite of Ms. Ryan's injurious and slanderous accusations, Ms. Sanders offered to bake her a pie—accompanied by a #fakenews hashtag. Ms. Ryan added insult to injury by telling Ms. Sanders she would decline a slice of the chocolate pecan pie.

"Okay I want to watch you bake it and put it on the table," she tweeted. "But forgive me, I won't eat it. Remember you guys don't like the press."

Perhaps Ms. Ryan was familiar with that infamous pie scene from *The Help* and feared it might spark another viral hashtag: "Two-Slice Hilly."

JESUS, CHEERLEADERS, AND DODGE COUNTY, GEORGIA

You would be hard-pressed to find anybody in Dodge County, Georgia, who does not stand for the national anthem or take a knee to pray. That's just how it is.

So when the Dodge County High School cheerleaders started selling T-shirts that read, "In Dodge County, we stand for the flag, kneel for the cross," nobody thought it would cause a controversy. But, sweet mercy, did it cause a stink.

Dodge County School Board member Shirley Ikedionwu posted a scathing message on Facebook calling the shirts "politically divisive."[13]

"This shirt is not only one-sided but offensive," she wrote. "I can't imagine how our children would feel entering a place that is supposed to be welcoming and accepting of students from all walks of life, beliefs, and perspectives—but instead, they are faced with this type of exclusionary message."

---

13 Todd Starnes, "Todd Starnes: T-shirts Saying 'Stand for the Flag, Kneel for the Cross' Draw Protest at School, Fox News, August 17, 2018, https://www.foxnews.com/opinion/todd-starnes-t-shirts-saying-stand-for-the-flag-kneel-for-the-cross-draw-protest-at-school.

Proceeds from the patriotic shirts were going to help fund cheerleading competitions. But that did not seem to satisfy the school board member's anger. Ikedionwu wrote that she personally contacted school system administrators to voice her concerns.

"At this point, the shirt will no longer be sold," she declared.

But that's when local residents and businesses got involved and decided to sell the T-shirts off campus.

"I'm standing because it has the United States flag on it and the cross. Those are two things I will back any day of the week," said Nikki Mullis, the manager of White Hat Auto in Eastland.

Mullis, who was a guest on my radio show, said that people are calling to purchase shirts from across the world. They even shipped three shirts to Afghanistan.

"This ain't just Georgia anymore," she said. "We are a community that when something happens we are all together."

Credit manager Amanda Parker tells me never in a million years would she have thought there would be a controversy over Old Glory and the Lord.

"We are just a small town in Eastman, Georgia, and we're standing up for our Christian faith and what we believe in," she said.

But there were some folks around town who were triggered by the patriotic message.

"It stands for the hurt of black people getting killed, beat by police officers and getting off with it," one resident told television station WMAZ.[14] "So therefore, we as black people, some of us have taken that, to us, that's what it looks like."

14 Pepper Baker, "T-shirts Cause Controversy in Dodge County," 13 WMAZ, August 15, 2018, https://www.13wmaz.com/article/news/local/t-shirts-cause-controversy-in-dodge-county/93-584487596.

To be clear, there is nothing on the shirt that comes even close to promoting police brutality.

"I don't see anything wrong with that shirt," resident Bill Tripp told me. "The South is known for being the Bible Belt. If you can't stand for the flag and you can't stand for the cross—I don't know what you can stand for."

I reckon there are more than a few folks around Dodge County who would offer an "amen" at that sentiment.

HEY OBAMA, KISS MY GRITS

When President Obama promised to fundamentally transform America, we had no idea he was secretly plotting to ban biscuits and grits.

The 2010 Healthy Hunger-Free Kids Act strictly limited calories, fat, salt, sugar, and just about everything else that makes food edible—including grits. It was the War of Culinary Aggression.

"We could originally serve half whole grains but that changed in 2012 when we had to start serving one hundred percent whole grains," said Stephanie Dillard, the child nutrition director for Geneva County Schools in Alabama. That meant no more grits.

"And grits are a staple in the South," Ms. Dillard told me. "Students really want to eat their grits."

I'm fairly certain that, had Southerners known President Obama had taken away their biscuits and grits, Mitt Romney would've won the South in a landslide.

My New York editor just sent me an email reminding me that I have a diverse readership, and I should probably include a working definition of the word "grits." The word "diverse" is a polite way of saying I have a number of Yankee readers.

So for all y'all up in the Bronx, grits are made from stone-ground corn and prepared with lots of butter. Grits are also versatile—meaning you can eat them for breakfast or supper (which is the meal called dinner north of the Mason-Dixon Line).

"Grits and fish go well together," Ms. Dillard said. "Students love that."

Of course, the folks from South Carolina are renowned for shrimp and grits, and I know a few folks in Mississippi who toss a few eggs in theirs. I'm from Tennessee, and we prefer a little cheese in our grits—but I digress.

The Obama administration also had a problem with traditional Southern buttermilk biscuits made from Martha White flour.

"Biscuits have to be one hundred percent whole grain," Ms. Dillard said. "It's not the kind of biscuit you would see at a restaurant."

Nor is it the kind of biscuit you would see on your grandmother's dining room table or a Wednesday night church supper. Why, no self-respecting Southerner would ever serve such an atrocity.

I had the unfortunate experience of eating one of those government-approved biscuits. I wouldn't wish that culinary apostasy on Bernie Sanders.

"It's hard to find good, fluffy, one hundred-percent whole grain biscuits," Ms. Dillard told me.

I'm not terribly surprised. The South has a better chance of rising than a 100-percent whole grain, government-approved biscuit.

"The students have gotten used to them," she said. "They really aren't that bad."

My friend, the Southern humorist Shellie Rushing Tomlinson, seems to think whole grain biscuits are a Communist plot.

"No freedom-honoring nation should force whole grain cat-head biscuits on their young," she told me.

Like Grandmother Starnes used to say, biscuits should only be made from buttermilk and Martha White flour, the way the Good Lord intended.

All that to say, a delegation of school nutritionists recently paid a visit to Congress to politely inform lawmakers that the Obama-era food rules were overcooking their grits.

"We're asking for some flexibility so we can serve fifty-percent whole grains," Ms. Dillard said. "If we can have that, we would be allowed to serve our grits."

The School Nutrition Association is lobbying for a relaxation of the rules too. But they took me to task for saying President Obama had banned grits.

"There's no ban on one kind of food—it just has to fit within the criteria," their spokesperson told me.

Grits don't fit into their criteria, so in my estimation that means they're banned.

For what it's worth, Miss Shellie stands with the good people of Alabama as they try to bring back grits.

"May God have favor on their efforts," she said. "Grits can heal America."

We now ask Democrats and Republicans in Congress to do the right thing and restore biscuits and grits to their rightful place. And the next time the federal government decides to outlaw basic Southern provisions, We the People should rise up and tell Uncle Sam to kiss our grits.

FIRST THEY CAME FOR DAISY DUKE, THEN THEY CAME FOR THE GENERAL LEE

If you still doubt there is a full-fledged cultural cleansing of the Southern states, consider the plight of the beloved General Lee (from *The Dukes of Hazzard*, not the Civil War.)

Warner Brothers announced they will remove the Confederate Flag from atop one of the most famous cars in television history. They will also ban any Dukes of Hazzard merchandise that once sported the Confederate flag.

Maybe they could just paint a rainbow flag on top and rename it the General Sherman. He culturally cleansed the South too. Just ask the good people of Atlanta.

Sears, Walmart, and eBay have also announced they will no longer sell Confederate merchandise. And that could explain why Sears is on life support.

Meanwhile, lawmakers are debating whether to remove state flags and rename schools and parks and streets named after Confederate war heroes. In Washington, DC, they're talking about removing Confederate statues from the US Capitol. Senator Mitch McConnell wants a statue of Jefferson Davis evicted from the Kentucky statehouse. And Senator Harry Reid wants UNLV to rename its Runnin' Rebels mascot.

It's only a matter of time before the cultural revolutionaries literally destroy films like *Forrest Gump* and burn copies of *Tom Sawyer* and *Huckleberry Finn.* Stalin and Lenin would be bursting with pride.

And mark my words: the Left's cultural crusade will not stop with the Confederate Flag. They will use the perception of racism and hatred to whitewash history and silence dissent.

And one day—very soon—I predict they will come after another flag: the one with broad stripes and bright stars. So don't be terribly surprised when even Republicans stand idly by as they burn the Star-Spangled Banner.

Run Forrest, run.

19

IT'S THE END OF THE WORLD AS WE KNOW IT

FORMER PRESIDENT OBAMA once said people who cling to their guns and religion are bitter Americans. Former secretary of state Hillary Clinton called us a basket of deplorables. And Joe Biden once called us the dregs of society.

The mainstream media and the ruling class treat those of us who cherish freedom and liberty like lepers—outcasts. They preach from the gospel of civility but mock us with disdain and condescension.

"They're too stupid," said HBO host Bill Maher on TBS. "They're like a dog."

John Hickenlooper, the Democratic mayor of Denver, called us "backward thinkers."

Actress Janeane Garofalo called the Tea Party racist saying, "This is racism straight up and is nothing but a bunch of teabagging rednecks."

Attorney General Eric Holder called us a "nation of cowards," and First Lady Michelle Obama said, "For the first time in my adult life I am proud of my country."

Perhaps one of the most telling examples of this hatred toward our nation came from an Obama nominee to the federal court, Judge Edward Chen. The following paragraphs appeared in the *Washington Times* in 2009:

> Judge Chen's words speak for themselves. When the congregation sang "America the Beautiful" at a funeral, Judge Chen told the audience of his "feelings of ambivalence and cynicism when confronted with appeals to patriotism—sometimes I cannot help but feel that there are too much [*sic*] injustice and too many inequalities that prevent far too many Americans from enjoying the beauty extolled in that anthem."
>
> In a speech on Sept. 22, 2001, he said that among his first responses to the Sept. 11 terrorist attacks on America was a "sickening feeling in my stomach about what might happen to race relations and religious tolerance on our own soil. ...One has to wonder whether the seemingly irresistible forces of racism, nativism and scapegoating which has [*sic*] recurred so often in our history can be effectively restrained."[1]

When I hear people sing "America the Beautiful," I have feelings of gratitude and thanksgiving that God would shed his grace on a people so undeserving.

---

1 The Washington Times, "EDITORIAL: Another Judicial Radical," *Washington Times*, October 25, 2009, https://www.washingtontimes.com/news/2009/oct/25/another-judicial-radical/.

Paula Deen knows about that grace. One of the most wonderfully kind and generous chefs in the nation had a difficult lot in life. She's been a guest on my radio show several times over the years. She gives bear hugs and smells like a butter cookie.

"I didn't have two nickels to rub together," she told me. "So, it makes me very appreciative and very grateful for everything."

Miss Paula is proof anyone can achieve the American dream. "I have worked hard. But God, in turn, has blessed that hard work. And it's important that when we're blessed that we pay it forward and try to help someone else."

It's that type of spirit that built a nation—a nation of free men and women who trusted God and not the government. If you believe liberal lawmakers and the mainstream media, we are a nation who no longer believes in God. But that's just not true.

Former Congressman Randy Forbes, a Republican from the Commonwealth of Virginia and chairman of the Congressional Prayer Caucus, addressed this very issue in *U.S. News & World Report*.

> So, if America was birthed upon Judeo-Christian principles, at what point in time did our nation cease to be Judeo-Christian? It was not when a small minority tried to remove the name of God from our public buildings and monuments. It was not when they tried to remove God from our veterans' flag folding ceremonies or to take the motto off our coins. Nor was it when this small minority fought to banish prayer from our schools, strip the 10 Commandments from our

> courtrooms or remove the phrase "one nation under God" from the new Capitol Visitor Center.
>
> No, the answer is clear: While America has always welcomed individuals of diverse faiths and non-faith, we have never ceased to be a Judeo-Christian nation. That small minority could tear references of faith off every building and document across our nation, but it would not change the fact that we were built on Judeo-Christian principles.[2]

According to Gallup, 78 percent of Americans consider themselves Christian. So what does that tell us?

It tells us President Obama was off the mark when he told the Christian Broadcasting Network in 2007 that the United States was "no longer just a Christian nation." On the contrary, Mr. President, the United States is overwhelmingly a Christian nation.

Friends, I hope you know that Christ alone is the author of our freedom. Without Him, without His guiding hand, our nation will cease being free.

Throughout my travels across this great nation, I've discovered some wonderful people—my fellow countrymen.

I've met police officers and firefighters, nurses and school teachers. I've met soldiers and veterans, Boy Scouts and Girl Scouts. I've met pastors and journalists, farmers and construction workers.

I've watched them pledge allegiance to the flag, to one nation under God. I've heard their stories of defending our nation from

---

2 J. Randy Forbes, "Obama Is Wrong When He Says We're Not a Judeo-Christian Nation," *U.S. News & World Report*, May 7, 2009, https://www.usnews.com/opinion/articles/2009/05/07/obama-is-wrong-when-he-says-were-not-a-judeo-christian-nation.

the Halls of Montezuma to the shore of Tripoli. They go to work. They go to church. They go hunting and fishing. They go to Little League games and Sunday dinners-on-the-ground.

I've watched the sun rise over Egg Harbor Township in New Jersey and watched the sunset over the Golden Gate Bridge in San Francisco. I've taken a riverboat ride on the mighty Mississippi and climbed the Great Smoky Mountains.

I've had barbecue in Memphis and gumbo in New Orleans, deep dish pizza in Chicago and a hot dog from a street cart in New York City. I've dined on Moon Pies in Chattanooga and Sonora dogs in Tucson.

I've watched a stick ball game in Brooklyn and a baseball game in Atlanta. I've run the New York City Marathon and welcomed in the new year in Times Square.

This is the America I know. This is the America I love.

But our nation and our world are at a precarious point in history. Many folks, Christian and non-Christian, are asking the same question: What is this world coming to?

According to the Bible, this world is coming to an end. For generations, we've heard the prophecies—earthquakes, fires, floods, famine, wars. There is turmoil and unrest in the land. There is sadness and sorrow, a sense of hopelessness seems to grip the country. But friends, as I write these words, I do so with a heart filled with joy. That's because this world is not my home. And if you are a believer in Jesus Christ, it's not your home either. We're just passing through.

The Bible calls us aliens in this world. The aliens are people who have placed their hope and their trust in Jesus Christ. There's a song made famous by R.E.M. called, "It's the End of the World as We Know It." There's a bit of truth in that tune. It is the end of the world as we know it. And you know something? I feel just fine.

When I was a little boy growing up in the South, I walked down the aisle of a Southern Baptist church and accepted Jesus Christ as my Lord and Savior. Romans 10:13 tells us that those who "call upon the name of the Lord shall be saved."

And one day, perhaps very soon, Jesus is going to return to take His people home. One of my favorite gospel songs talks about a "Great, Gettin' Up Morning." And on that glorious day, I don't know about you, but I plan on getting up and going somewhere.

20

I'VE READ THE BOOK, AND I KNOW HOW IT ENDS

Anderson Cooper: This is breaking news on CNN. Strange events are happening across the country both in the sky and on the ground. New York City's 9-1-1 system was overwhelmed just moments ago by complaints of loud horn sections blasting across the boroughs. We tried to reach city officials but were unable to hear their responses because of what sounded like trumpets sounding in the distance. Civil Defense sirens have sounded in most American cities, and people are being urged to take shelter immediately. Live on the phone with us is General John Bigguns from NORAD. Sir, what can you tell us?

General Bigguns: Anderson—we've never seen anything like it. Our radar systems are overwhelmed right now. We're tracking hundreds, if not thousands of targets.

Anderson Cooper: Dear Lord! Are we all doomed? Which cities will be hit first?

General Bigguns: Uh, I think you might have misunderstood, Anderson. These aren't incoming targets.

Anderson Cooper: I'm confused, General.

General Bigguns: Anderson—these are outbound targets.

Anderson Cooper: We'll get back to the general in just a few moments, but right now, I want to bring in Dr. Rashad Guppie—CNN's chief environmental reporter. According to eyewitness accounts, the clouds are rolling back, and it appears the sky is opening. Got any answers for us?

Dr. Guppie: Anderson, it's pretty obvious what is happening. Former vice president Al Gore has just released a statement, and he believes the parting of the clouds is a direct result of climate change. Mr. Gore said it's imperative Americans immediately reduce their carbon footprint.

Anderson Cooper: Certainly makes sense to me, Dr. Guppie. In the meantime, let's go live to Washington, DC, where our Token Blonde Reporter is standing by.

Token Blonde Reporter: Anderson, I'm at the Tomb of the Unknown Soldier, and I've gotta tell you—my surgically enhanced body is shivering all over. Just moments ago, the ground started shaking, and the grave markers began falling over.

Anderson Cooper: An earthquake, Token Blonde Reporter?

Token Blonde Reporter: That's what I thought at first, Anderson. But then—the lids on the coffins started opening up and…

Anderson Cooper: Tell us, Token Blonde Reporter. Tell us what you see.

Token Blonde Reporter: (hushed voice) Anderson, I see dead people—and I think they're alive.

Anderson Cooper: I don't mean to interrupt you, but now we're getting reports of breaking news on board the Space Shuttle Endeavor. Let's listen in to this live feed from the Johnson Space Center in Houston.

Endeavor: Uh Houston, we've got a problem.

Houston: All systems appear to be functioning normally, Endeavor.

Endeavor: It's not mechanical, Houston. We're picking up some unidentified flying objects.

Houston: Could you repeat that Endeavor? Your last transmission was a bit garbled. Sounded like you said there were some UFOs flying around up there.

Endeavor: Affirmative, Houston. Unidentified flying objects—and there are a lot of them.

Houston: You boys drinking something up there?

Endeavor: That's a negative, Houston. The objects appear to be human in nature and seem to be fairly docile. We've observed many of them smiling and—SWEET MERCY Houston!

Houston: What is it Endeavor? What's going on up there?

Endeavor: I could've sworn I just saw Billy Graham floating by the shuttle bay. He was holding a sign.

Houston: A sign? What did it say?

Endeavor: "I told you so."

Anderson Cooper: Obviously, something delusional is happening on board the shuttle. We will keep you posted. We're also monitoring developments overseas in Europe. Correspondent Jacques LePew is live in Paris. Jacques?

Jacques: Bonjour, Anderson. Seems like a normal day in gay Paris! Nothing out of zee ordinary to report.

Anderson Cooper: Thanks, Jacques. We're getting similar reports from London, Moscow, and most of Western Europe. We've also tried reaching out to some of the nation's religious leaders, but so far, no one has returned our calls. Wait just a moment—I'm being told the president is about to address the nation. Let's go live to the White House.

POTUS: My fellow Americans, we are witnessing extraordinary events across the nation. There are reports of citizens simply vanishing into thin air—of four massive creatures on horses galloping across the plains of Texas. It's unclear what's behind the disappearances, but you can rest easy knowing that the top minds in my government are on top of this. My team is fired up and ready to go. So far, most of the disappearances have occurred in the South, Midwest, and Texas. Most of our major cities—Los Angeles, San Francisco, Seattle, and New York—are unscathed. At this point, I believe it is prudent to stay home, listen to the instructions of your local authorities, and find solace with a politically correct, government-sanctioned deity. Thank you, and may the aforementioned politically correct, government-sanctioned deity bless America.

Anderson Cooper: I believe we now have a reporter set to go live from Times Square. Do we have the shot? Excellent. Let's go live to Times Square and reporter Todd Starnes. (Silence)

Anderson Cooper: Todd?

Anderson Cooper: Todd?

Anderson Cooper: Todd?

Anderson Cooper: My apologies, ladies and gentlemen. But I'm being told Todd has been caught up in the moment. But all the rest of us in the CNN newsroom are still here. We'll be right back after this break.

21

THE SHINING CITY UPON A HILL

PRESIDENT BIDEN PROMISED Americans that his administration would usher in a dark winter across the land of the free and home of the brave. He delivered on that campaign promise. It has been an insidious darkness. We are standing at the edge of the abyss.

I received a telephone call from a listener just after the Biden inauguration. He feared that Lady Liberty's lamp was flickering. He worried that America would never again be the shining city on a hill that President Reagan and President Kennedy once foretold.

Many folks are surprised when I tell them that the Great Communicator and JFK actually borrowed that phrase from a famous speech delivered by John Winthrop aboard a ship bound for Massachusetts.

The great Puritan leader called on the people to set an example for the rest of the world. The speech was titled, "A Model of Christian Charity." And it was part inspirational and part warning.

"For we must consider that we shall be as a city upon a hill. The eyes of all people are upon us. So that if we shall deal falsely with our God in this work we have undertaken, and so cause

Him to withdraw His present help from us, we shall be made a story and a by-word through the world," he said.

JFK, then president-elect, invoked Winthrop's ideology during an address at the state house in Boston in 1961:

> But I have been guided by the standard John Winthrop set before his shipmates on the flagship *Arbella* three hundred and thirty-one years ago, as they, too, faced the task of building a new government on a perilous frontier.
>
> "We must always consider," he said, "that we shall be as a city upon a hill—the eyes of all people are upon us."
>
> Today the eyes of all people are truly upon us—and our governments, in every branch, at every level, national, state and local, must be as a city upon a hill—constructed and inhabited by men aware of their great trust and their great responsibilities.
>
> For we are setting out upon a voyage in 1961 no less hazardous than that undertaken by the Arabella in 1630. We are committing ourselves to tasks of statecraft no less awesome than that of governing the Massachusetts Bay Colony, beset as it was then by terror without and disorder within.
>
> History will not judge our endeavors—and a government cannot be selected—merely on the basis of color or creed or even party affiliation.

> Neither will competence and loyalty and stature, while essential to the utmost, suffice in times such as these.[1]

It's quite remarkable how the words of a man of God delivered in 1630 to the future citizens of the Massachusetts Bay Colony could be so relevant and quite frankly, prophetic today.

"Beloved, there is now set before us life and death, good and evil," in that we are commanded this day to love the Lord our God, and to love one another, to walk in his ways and to keep his Commandments and his ordinance and his laws, and the articles of our Covenant with Him, that we may live and be multiplied, and that the Lord our God may bless us in the land whither we go to possess it."

Winthrop then offered a warning to his congregation—one that modern-day Americans should heed.

"But if our hearts shall turn away, so that we will not obey, but shall be seduced, and worship other Gods, our pleasure and profits, and serve them; it is propounded unto us this day, we shall surely perish out of the good land whither we pass over this vast sea to possess it."

I told the caller that day I do still have hope in our great nation. I believe we can step back from the abyss. And I believe that we can once again be that shining city on a hill. Yes, America can turn from its wickedness. But will we have the courage to do so?

---

1 John F. Kennedy, "Address of President-Elect John F. Kennedy Delivered to a Joint Convention of the General Court of the Commonwealth of Massachusetts, January 9, 1961," John F. Kennedy Presidential Library and Museum, January 9, 1961, https://www.jfklibrary.org/archives/other-resources/john-f-kennedy-speeches/massachusetts-general-court-19610109.

Winthrop extolled his congregants to be courageous and to "choose life." And in doing so, "that we and our seed may live, by obeying His voice and cleaving to Him, for He is our life and our prosperity."

And that's why I wrote this book—to stir the hearts and the minds of my fellow countrymen that we might rise up against the forces of darkness that have occupied our land. That we would have the courage to stand up to the critical race theorists, the alphabet activists, the professional race grifters, and the godless heathen atheists.

I wrote this book so that God-loving patriots would no longer be silent in the face of evil.

In his final address to the nation, President Reagan emboldened us to remember the words of the Pilgrims who settled these shores:

> And that's about all I have to say tonight, except for one thing. The past few days when I've been at that window upstairs, I've thought a bit of the "shining city upon a hill." The phrase comes from John Winthrop, who wrote it to describe the America he imagined. What he imagined was important because he was an early Pilgrim, an early freedom man. He journeyed here on what today we'd call a little wooden boat; and like the other Pilgrims, he was looking for a home that would be free. I've spoken of the shining city all my political life, but I don't know if I ever quite communicated what I saw when I said it. But in my mind it was a tall, proud city built on rocks stronger than oceans, wind-swept, God-blessed, and teeming with people of all kinds living in harmony and peace; a

> city with free ports that hummed with commerce and creativity. And if there had to be city walls, the walls had doors and the doors were open to anyone with the will and the heart to get here. That's how I saw it, and see it still. And how stands the city on this winter night? More prosperous, more secure, and happier than it was 8 years ago. But more than that: After 200 years, two centuries, she still stands strong and true on the granite ridge, and her glow has held steady no matter what storm. And she's still a beacon, still a magnet for all who must have freedom, for all the pilgrims from all the lost places who are hurtling through the darkness, toward home. We've done our part. And as I walk off into the city streets, a final word to the men and women of the Reagan revolution, the men and women across America who for 8 years did the work that brought America back. My friends: We did it. We weren't just marking time. We made a difference. We made the city stronger, we made the city freer, and we left her in good hands. All in all, not bad, not bad at all.[2]

That is the America imagined by Winthrop and JFK and Reagan. A strong nation. A free nation. A Christian nation. And that is the America I imagine today.

But now we are living in difficult days—days foretold in the Holy Bible of persecution in the land. But we must not let our hearts be troubled.

---

2 "Farewell Address to the Nation," Ronald Reagan Presidential Library & Museum, January 11, 1989, https://www.reaganlibrary.gov/archives/speech/farewell-address-nation

As President John Adams wrote to his wife, Abigail, in 1776, "Yet through all the gloom I can see the rays of ravishing Light and Glory."

Adams and his fellow revolutionaries and their families were facing certain death at the hands of the Red Coats. Yet there was joy in his heart because he knew that his Redeemer lived.

And so, too, must modern-day patriots be courageous and cling to the truth that the Light will one day dispel Biden's darkness.

Like previous generations, we, too, must stand in faith with a firm reliance on the protection of Divine Providence. We must pledge to each other our lives, our fortunes, and our sacred honor.

We must once again affirm that the truths we hold to be self-evident, that all men are created equal, that they are endowed by their Creator with certain unalienable rights, that among these are life, liberty, and the pursuit of happiness.

Rights given to us not by the Democrat Party or the Republican Party or the Libertarians. Rights given to us by Almighty God.

In closing, I call on all free men and women, all lovers of American Liberty, joyful warriors all, to join me in a prayerful petition to the Supreme Judge of the World just as our forefathers did so many years ago.

May God Save the United States of America.